Seize the Green Day:
Rock and Roll Hall of Fame Edition!

Written & Edited by Niki Lee
Illustrated by Alex Langenstein
Back Cover: Eleonora Gatti
Copyright 2015

Photo: Kerry Harris

1

Seize the Green Day/1

Green Day Is:

Mike Dirnt./16

Tré Cool/19

Jason White/22

Jason Freese/24

Jeff Matika/26

Bill Schneider/27

Billie Joe Armstrong/29

The Beatles/40

Lost Wages/42

American Idiot Front-to-Back/45

On The Boardwalk in Atlantic City/53

Oh Baltimore/57

The Chunnel/64

Pit Tactics/66

We're Not Gonna Take It/70

2

Waffles and Mud/74

Willkomen/81

Au Revoir/82

Back in the USA/83

Atlantic City Redux/85

Bullet in a Bible/89

File Under Favorites/92

Death & Resurrection/97

3

Photographers/100

Alex Langenstein/108

How *Seize the Green Day* Landed in the Rock and Roll Hall of Fame/110

Rock and Roll Hall of Fame Pre-Induction/114

Rock and Roll Hall of Fame Induction Week, Cleveland/177

Live at the House of Blues- Act 1 -- Sweet Children/188

Live at the House of Blues- Act 2 -- Green Day/193

My Trip to Cleveland:
Part 1/197
Part 2/208
Part 3/218

More Stuff.../231

Special Thanks to Donors/252

A Cutty Named J., me, Alex's Bar, Long Beach, California, 2008. Photo: "Shanty" Cheryl Groff

Seize the Green Day

I am a 52-year-old punk rock groupie who entered the fold at 45.

45.

Do the math and you will find JFK hadn't been elected president when I appeared on this earth. Eisenhower held that title on June 9th, 1959.

As the second half of my century begins, I can't help but get misty as I look at a pair of dirt-covered Chucks hanging from the closet door of my West Hollywood bedroom in my West Hollywood apartment in, um, West Hollywood, California.

Over them it reads, Belgian Mud, 2005. That means on July 1, 2005, I was in the middle of a muddy mosh pit at the Rock Werchter Music Festival in Leuven, Belgium. I was dancing to the music of Green Day. It was one of seven Green Day shows I'd see in Europe and America as the band toured in support of their dazzling new album, *American Idiot.*

I'm not sure how that would strike Billie Joe Armstrong, Mike Dirnt and Tré Cool, the three musicians who catapulted me out of whatever I thought about middle-age. My transformation from hermit-like suburbanite to world-traveling geek was stunning. The first time I heard that pissed-off riff of the title song, my whole body surged backwards in my black swivel chair, hands involuntarily flying off the computer keyboard shot full of electricity.

Who the hell was writing great music?!?

Before Green Day and *American Idiot* converted me into a full-on freaky fan, I was a shut-in. Having never learned basic socialization skills from my mentally ill parents, I've had to unravel most of life's challenges on my own. Difficult as that continues to be, it's made me independent and that's a good thing. That small germ of self-determination has helped me out of many a twisted moment.

It was quite handy when I had to pull myself back from the brink of becoming a sloppy drug addict with severe health, relationship and job problems. The never-ending pain of sciatica got me tethered to painkillers and Bailey's Irish Cream. I then had a marathon eating binge of Cocoa Puffs & whole milk with packs of Camel Lights on the side. I could barely walk which only increased my every day anxiety and depression.

I'd wake up at five a.m., wander to my computer in my pajamas to do my job, light up a cigarette, pour myself a huge mug of ¾ Bailey's and ¼ hot chocolate, pop a pain pill and top it off with a Xanax.

Later, I found it expeditious to pour the Bailey's directly onto the cereal, skipping the milk altogether. I'd be drunk by 11 a.m. crawling back into bed to sleep it off. When none of my clothes fit, visits to the liquor store became embarrassingly frequent and my paper recycling bin was filled with too many empty boxes of that *Cuckoo for Cocoa Puffs* bird, I saw the light. In March 2004, I put myself on a 30-day rehab plan and got off everything. I'd read in some self-help book that *"IT ONLY TAKES 30 DAYS TO CHANGE A BAD HABIT! YOU CAN DO IT!"*

Instead of a bottle of Bailey's, I'd buy a yoga magazine. Instead of lighting up, I'd make myself go for a walk. It sucked in the beginning but I kept at it. The more I read, the more interested I became in yoga. It saved me and my back.

I injured my lower back in 1985 before a singing gig. I grabbed an amp that someone loaned me and I didn't realize how heavy it was until I tried to lift it. When I did, I dropped to the floor. Ever since, that herniated disc has provided chronic pain.

Practicing yoga mended wounds and helped me socialize. It threw me into situations where I *had* to interact with others; like having to put my purple yoga mat less than six-inches from someone else's sweaty butt.

I tried to hide in the back of the class, but, sensing my terror, one instructor thought it a good idea to toss my mat in the middle of the class. Sink or swim.

Swimming is good.

A month of changing my behavior and I was able to break off the miserable relationship. I got a couple of tattoos and started over in April.

In 2004, the U.S. was in the throes of retro-homogenization. And yet, Green Day outwitted corporate bullshit and right-wing politics to produce a masterpiece. They weren't afraid to say "fuck you" to the *powers that be*. I hadn't realized how much I'd been craving that kind of expression and I wasn't alone.

Where did I first hear this opus? Why, on the Howard Stern Show of course! It's a well-documented fact that the majority of middle-aged, middle-class women are dedicated Howard fans. "And, a Baba Booey to y'all."

I headed to my local Record & Tape Traders to get the CD and was surprised to find an angry sales clerk who didn't want to sell it to me.

"What? Why?" I asked.
Tapping the CD he said, "*Major label.*"
"What the hell does that mean?" I asked.

When Green Day was coming up in the 1990s Bay area, they rattled chains after signing with Warner Bros.

Punk philosophy frowns upon signing with corporate labels: everything's *DIY.* But, when you're a working musician and you've grown beyond yourself, why pass up an opportunity to get someone with resources to pay for your work? Hey, I hate corporations. That's why I like Elvis Costello's take: it's very punk to use a corporations' money to make art that undermines its' agenda.

And fun, too!!

Billie Joe, Mike and Tré swiftly outpaced their peers as well as older musicians. It didn't fly. People got jealous. People got angry. To this day, the media, and other dullards, harp on the band's record deal, *two decades ago!* With over 20 years of success, critically, financially and culturally, Green Day walks the razor's edge between commercial success and punk aesthetics quite well.

"Gimme that album!" I said, snatching the CD out of his hand.

"She's holding on my heart..."
Green Day fan Katie McPansy Grogan

I bought a copy for myself and then copies for anyone who was interested and even for those who weren't. My guitar students, *The Hollow Minds,* all got copies. A whole community of future rock stars was turned on to Green Day whether their parents liked it or not.

My guitar students: *The Hollow Minds, 2007.*
Back: Max Carlson, Reiter Boldt, Dillon Hannah, Ricky Kneebone. Front: me, Leigha Crowell.
Photos on both pages: Mary Kate Hannah

THE HOLLOW MINDS

(on my solid ankle)

I listened to *American Idiot* like a mental patient for a year. It's brutal beauty: honest and poignant. Pure genius.

Furious guitars, insanely catchy pop melodies and searing lyrics make this album one of the greatest of all time. Not to mention the themes of isolation, anger, love, lust, betrayal, and just for kicks, death and resurrection.

An album called *American Idiot*? Jesus, that takes balls!

The first shows I went to in 2004 were empty compared to the band's summer shows in 2005 as news of the album erupted around the world. Green Day had been languishing for several years. They even considered calling it quits. When master tapes for a new album, *Cigarettes and Valentines*, were "stolen," they saw an opportunity to get risky and try something different. That difference launched them into a second wave of popularity after their first ride in 1994 with the release of their album *Dookie*.

Admittedly, I didn't know much about the band before *American Idiot*. I had a vague recollection of them as being irreverent, tuneful and having a brash cockiness. Someone put it perfectly, "They're like three kittens from the same litter."

Photos Kerry Harris

Mike Dirnt

Billie Joe Armstrong

Tré Cool

In the 90s, if I listened to music it was jazz; if I listened to radio it was talk. Hence, Howard Stern. That was pretty much it. At the time, I was married to a musical snob, a pianist/composer who'd laugh at the "three chord songs" I'd started to write. I didn't like him laughing at me so I got divorced and started playing gigs with my original songs.

1966

1979

1992

Photo: Trudy Slinger, 1999

Mid-decade, I did see a Green Day video on an awards show. Set in a mental institution, it was hilarious. I also remembered that one of the guys in the band had cool fuzzy brows over intense eyes. That's all I knew when *American Idiot* came along. And, hard as it is to comprehend, I didn't see the finale of *Seinfeld* until 10 years after it aired. I completely missed the phenomenon of *Good Riddance*, (Time of Your Life).

Green Day is:

MIKE DIRNT

Bassist Mike Dirnt is flawless. His beat is steady enough to withstand the force of tearing-ass from one side of an arena stage to the other. He's a childlike stoic; a badass rocker with a favorite number and a favorite color.

Mike was born Michael Ryan Pritchard. His early family life was rocky. He and Billie Joe met when they were 10. He loves his kids; he has two daughters and a son. He thinks it's great to be a dad because, "It gives me an excuse to watch cartoons." He's in a band called the Frustrators, stays trim and fit and has an affinity for high fashion.

Mike Dirnt by Beth Wieman.

Mike at 924 Gilman Street
with The Frustrators, 2-18-11.
Photo: Kerry Harris

Mike: by Beth Wieman

Tré Cool

It's slightly different with drummer Tré Cool. He's nuts! Born Frank Edwin Wright III, at any given time Tré will skip, dance, somersault or run around the stage in a frenzy. He's also known for smashing his drums and setting them on fire, climbing tall structures unassisted and taking over for talk-show hosts without permission. His hair is always swept into a whimsical peak of varying colors. Tré is a drum wizard and *NEVER* stops moving. Mid-tune, he effortlessly tosses drumsticks from his perch high-atop the stage. Maniacal fans dive after them. Colorful bras adorn the outside of his shirts and he's partial to riding crops.

Tré-isms: "I want to wash your grandmother."

"The album was very aggressive. It kicks you right in the balls."

"It has erections and everything!" (*American Idiot* on Broadway)

"I wanna survive an avalanche. I wanna be one of those people a dog finds buried under a ton of snow, almost dying of starvation."

"I never completed high school and I am very rich and very successful."

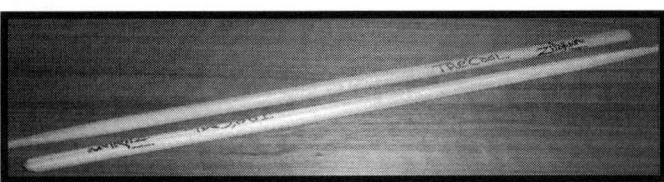

Eleonora Gatti's drumsticks.

Tré by Kerry Harris

"I can suck my own."
Tré Cool's entrance in Mainz, Germany.
Photo: Kerry Harris

Jason White

Green Day welcomed guitarist and vocalist Jason White in 1999. Hailing from Arkansas, he's an integral part of the band. He plays lead and takes over for their frontman throughout a Green Day show. When you look at the stage, you'll always find Jason on the left in his own spotlight, which, of course, he deserves.

Jason by Dorie Watts

Jason White & Katie McPansy Grogan

Jason White by Jimmy Douglas:
Future Daydream Photography

Jason Freese

Along with Mike, Tré and Jason, let us add Jason Freese. Jason F. plays sax, keyboards and sings with Green Day. He's a songwriter, record producer and recording engineer. And, a ham! He loves putting on various get-ups, coming center stage and blasting his sax into Billie Joe's...*package*.

Jason Freese & Billie Joe by Kimberly Martin.

Jason & fan Mary Rosenblatt

Jason White, Tré Cool & Jason Freese.
Photo: Jaymee Collier

Jeff Matika

Next up, Jeff Matika. Jeff is a friend of Jason White's from Little Rock, Arkansas. He's played in the bands Ashtray Babyhead and Magic Cropdusters. He's a guitarist, bassist and singer and was hand-picked to play with the band during their *21st Century Breakdown* tour. According to Jeff, "I like to stand behind Billie and Mike's amps."

Jeff Matika
Photo: Chris Dugan

BILL SCHNEIDER

Billie Joe, Babe, of Babe's Warehouse, and Bill Schneider by "Shanty" Cheryl Groff

Bill Schneider is omnipresent in the world of Green Day. He plays bass with Billie Joe and Jason White in the band Pinhead Gunpowder. He was Green Day's guitar tech for their *Nimrod* and *Warning* tours and he's been the band's tour manager since *American Idiot*. Mr. Schneider is also known as a "good explainer."

Bill Schneider with Pinhead Gunpowder.

Photos: Dorie Watts

THE SON OF RAGE AND LOVE:
BILLIE JOE ARMSTRONG

I'm not sure I've ever witnessed a force like Billie Joe Armstrong: lead singer, guitarist, lyricist, composer and outward conscience of Green Day. He is Charlie Chaplin. He is Jim Morrison. He is Mister Rogers. He is Elvis, John Lennon and Chrissie Hynde. And he is sex. He is exploding white light in his tight black rock-and-roll gear, spiked hair and perfectly smudged eyeliner -- an enlightened being wrapped up as a gigantic entertainer.

Photo: Kerry Harris

Kimberly Martin captures Billie Joe Armstrong playing a solo during *Minority*.

My first Green Day concert was Halloween 2004 at George Mason University. GMU is in Northern Virginia, an hour from where I lived in Catonsville, Maryland. The arena glowed with the blue cellphone lights of thousands of kids wired on adrenaline. I couldn't believe how excited *I* was. And, I was in the front row. Not the real front row, that's the mosh pit; a sacred ground for true believers. I was in the bleachers which was fine. No way was I flinging myself into a mass of pulsating teenagers. Although, it did look like fun.

While opening act New Found Glory played, I went outside to sell an extra ticket. When I got back, Green's Day's instruments had been set up. I saw Tré Cool's drums and got so excited! I mean, there they were! Right there!

My devotion only skyrocketed as the band took the stage. Billie Joe sprinted on wearing a devil's tail and horns. Several songs in, he took a dive into the swirling pit. It was cool until some guy grabbed his skinny red tie and started pulling him downward. From above, I could see the panic in his face as the tie got tighter. I was shocked. Didn't he know how famous he was? Wasn't he worried he might get killed?

Photo: Eleonora Gatti

Finally, a massive security guard waded into the melee, plucked Billie Joe from the madness and placed him gently back on stage. Unfazed, he ripped off the tie and continued singing his guts out.

That is so difficult. Do you know how difficult that is? Imagine it for a second. Did you do it? Hmmm...*OK*. All right. I trust you. I never saw him do that again; not in the next four years, anyway.

Photo: Kerry Harris

Photo: Kerry Harris

Tré sucking Billie Joe's thumb by Beth Wieman.

That October 31st, I found that a Green Day show is much more than a rock concert; it's a spectacle of lights, fire, confetti bombs, hijinx and nudity! Their performances have been called unparalleled: a mix of high-theater and pyrotechnics played out against a rock-and-roll backdrop.

Photo: Kerry Harris

With the crowd at its most fevered, Billie Joe launched into the song *Hitchin' a Ride*. As he did, he pushed his guitar to the side and slid his hand down the front of his pants. Then he put his other hand down the back of his pants, moaning and grinding. The crowd went wild. I put *my* hand to *my* mouth and laughed, "CAN HE DO THAT?!?" Suddenly he screamed, *"OH GOD! SOMEBODY FUCK ME!!"*

By the end of their set at G.M.U., I was drenched in sweat and voiceless from belting out Green Day songs I now knew by heart. As I lay awake that night, I ran over the experience in my mind and came to a startling conclusion: I had to see them again and that meant I had to travel.

I hated traveling. Traveling is good.

But, I had to trick myself into having fun at even the thought of traveling. Without any knowledge, I just believed that at the end of each anxiety-producing journey I'd take, there would be a show to look forward. And the shows would be with freaks like me in different places and with different accents.

A month later, I got a $1000 as back pay from a rip-off artist. The day I got the check, I noticed an online addition to Green Day's touring schedule: a show at The Hard Rock Hotel and Casino in Las Vegas on December 7, 2004. "I'll bet there are plenty of people who fly off just to see a concert if they want," I said to myself. "Maybe I could be one of those people." After all, this was no ordinary band, this was The Beatles.

Photo: Beth "Beffy" Wieman

Photo: Jaymee Collier

"OH GOD! SOMEBODY FUCK ME!"

Green Day at the L.A. Forum, August 25, 2009.
Photo: "Shanty" Cheryl Groff

Photo: Jaymee Collier

The Beatles!

My cousin Marty had a connection to the Beatles. He was the drummer for the 60s pop band, The Cyrkle and they were chosen as an opening for the Beatles during their historic 1966 American Tour. Beatles' manager Brian Epstein was even their manager for a while.

Marty eventually gave up music to become a bankruptcy attorney.

He hated talking about his experience with the Beatles. I managed to get some details out of him about the time he spent on the plane traveling with John, Paul, George and Ringo. *The F.F.* occupied the front of the plane, the press had the mid-section and the opening acts had the back. The Beatles and press were mobbed when they landed. By the time The Cyrkle deplaned, they deplaned to no one. Wah! Marty was very bitter about it. However, in my estimation, you put your ego on hold for the Beatles. That's that.

Things never took off for The Cyrkle. They didn't make any money. That's because their hits, *Red Rubber Ball* and *Turn Down Day,* were written by others. *Red Rubber Ball* was co-written by Paul Simon and *Turn Down Day* was written by David Blume. The Cyrkle also nixed the opportunity to record the Simon tune *59th Street Bridge Song* (Feelin' Groovy). And, that song went *Top 20!* in 1967.

The Beatles came to Washington, D.C., as part of the 1966 tour. I was six and lived about 20 minutes north of the city in Potomac, Maryland. Marty gave my parents two tickets to the show at D.C. Stadium.

Oh, my parents. They didn't even want to go! And neither one was brave enough to take just me. They were afraid of the city. They were afraid of everything. It wasn't fair. I loved the Beatles. I'd loved them ever since I danced to *I Should Have Known Better* when I was three.

Do you know what those two nitwits did? They went to the show and left *BEFORE* the Beatles played! They stayed for The Cyrkle and left. They complained that the screaming teenage girls hurt their ears. My parents were only in their early 30s; twenty years younger than I am today. When they got home and told me what they'd done, I trudged to my pink and white bedroom knowing I was on my own in the world

Lost Wages

Boarding the 747 to Las Vegas at Baltimore-Washington Airport on December 6, 2004, I panicked. I hated flying, especially after 9-11.

Mid-anxiety-attack, I remembered my pact to change. I forbade myself from being neurotic, if only for 36 hours.

The Las Vegas cab dropped me off at The Hard Rock Hotel and Resort around 8 p.m. that night. The place was all dressed up for a rock and roll Christmas. As the concierge put my papers in order, I pulled out my computerized e-ticket for Green Day's show the next night. Did I have the right thing, I asked? "Oh yeah, that's fine." Then he added, "The band just had a sound-check and they're wandering around the hotel." My knees buckled. (Sorry.) Concierge guy was correct, they were...wandering. I'd picked the correct hotel.

Stepping into the circular casino, I saw Mike Dirnt sitting alone at a roulette table. *Too scary for contact!* But, instead of running away, I took a breath, turned around and moved forward complimenting him on *American Idiot*. He was kind and asked my name as he shook my hand. God, that was cringey. Never again! I had nothing to say. I mean, really, what are you gonna say? I walked away as un-nervously as possible. It was much less stressful nodding to him as we passed each other in the hotel hallway the following day.

At the epicenter of the gaming room was the main bar. I ordered a long-neck Budweiser and kicked back on a red plastic-covered stool. I took in the scene. Billie Joe was at a craps table surrounded by drooling fans and very hefty security guards. I tried watching but this persistent airport executive kept yakking in my ear trying to make small-talk. Suddenly, Billie Joe bolted, running through the bar. It was hysterical watching those big security guys try to keep up with him. A moment later, Tré Cool strolled in wearing a hot pink silk shirt and white tie inside a grey suit. He looked every bit the conquering hero. I tried not to stare, but he was right in front of my stool!

Billie Joe came back to the craps table and airline executive was *still* talking. I didn't want to be rude but something had to be done. I opted for the truth. I told airline exec that what he and I were witnessing was akin to seeing the Beatles walking around a club in their heyday. I pointed to Billie Joe. "See that guy over there? He's John Lennon."

He said, "That guy over there, huh? He's like John Lennon?"

"Yep. I apologize for not really listening to what you were saying, but this is pretty historic stuff." I explained why I was in Las Vegas for only 36 hours. Intrigued, he decided to stay and watch. At 2 a.m., I conked out in my room.

American Idiot-Front-To-Back

At 5 p.m. the next afternoon, an *inside-the-hotel*-line for the show formed for hotel guests. There was another much, much longer line outside the club made up of teenagers and their parents. That line started gathering in the early a.m. To level the playing field, The Hard Rock let the inside and outside lines enter *The Joint* at the same time, making it semi-fair race-for-all to the front.

I made it.

My pit perspective.

I decided to enter the mosh pit for the first time. It was frightening, it was hot, it was sweaty, disgusting and liberating. Other peoples' wet hair stuck to my face and neck. Hands were searching everywhere. Guys were copping feels, girls were copping feels.

Crowd surfers tumbled overhead while violent men ran in circles beating the crap out of each other. We all danced so hard that at one point the entire standing crowd of 400 swayed all the way to the left, paused briefly, recovered slightly, then tipped all the way to the right. The only thing keeping us from collapsing into a crushed heap was the will to survive.

Awesome.

You'd think the pit would hurt my back, but no! You're so smashed against people it's actually like a full body massage. Sometimes your feet don't even touch the ground.

The show ended, the lights came up and I grabbed some red and white mangled Green Day confetti off the floor stuffing it into my pockets. God was I thirsty! My search for a drink was interrupted by bashing into a very tall, very handsome man. Seeing my Ramones T-shirt, he lifted me up and danced me around the room singing *I Wanna be Sedated.* He tripped trying to twirl me and we fell on the floor laughing.

Ramones guy bought me a beer and a Coke and we had an intense conversation. I excused myself for a moment to freshen up, after all, I was a mess from the pit. Upon my return, Ramones guy was a little *friendlier.* He put his hand on my ass and started looking at my, well, not my eyes.

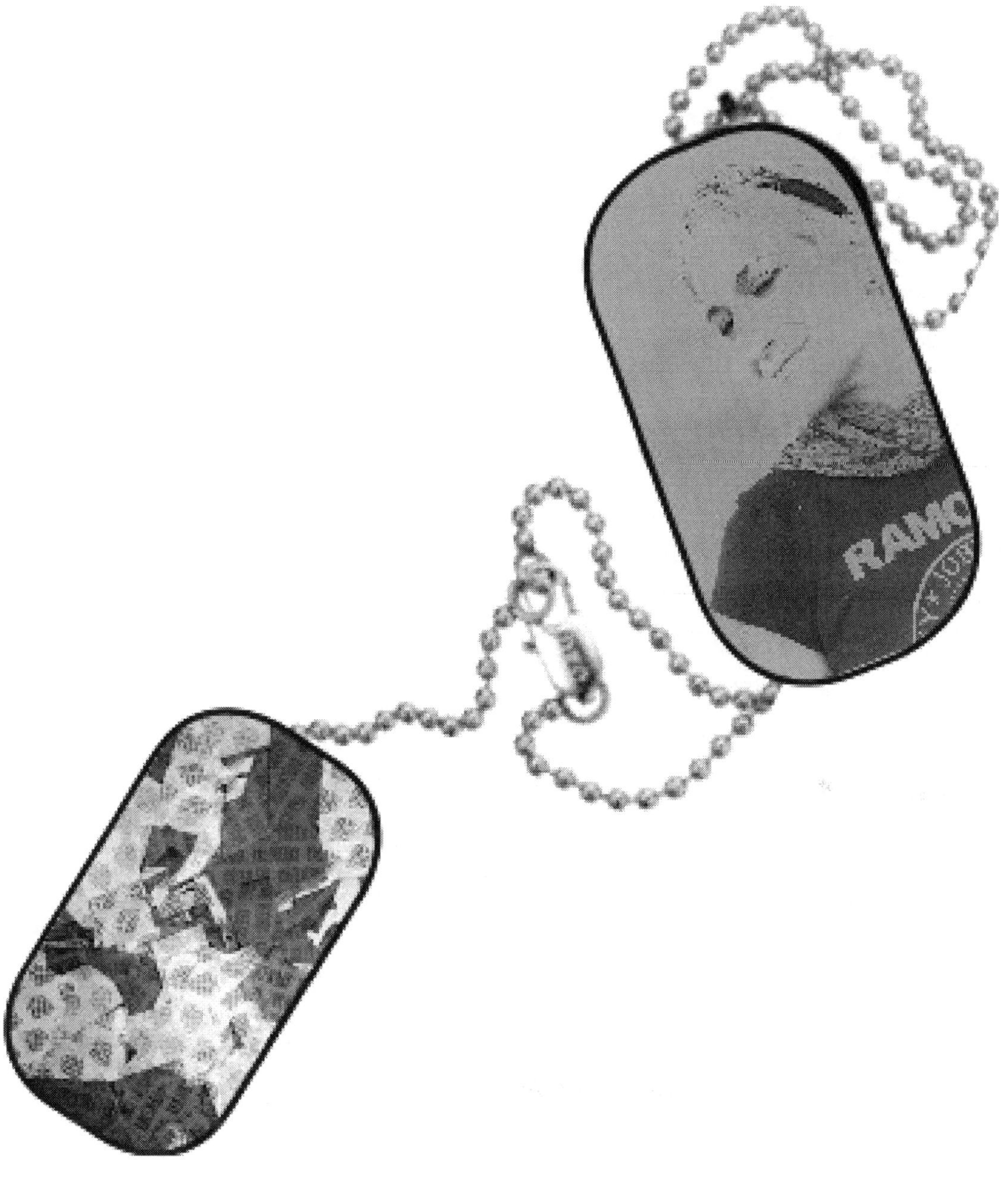

I took his hand off my ass, looked up and said, "That's right, they're real. Hey, where's the nice guy I was talking to a few minutes ago?"

"He got horny." Ramones guy replied.

"Can you bring him back?" I queried.

He insisted we do something after our drinks. Looking at the ring on his left finger I smiled, "It's two a.m., what exactly are we going to do?" He pressed on until I finally convinced him he was making a bad move. He shivered saying, "Oh my god! I was about to make such a *huge* mistake." Then he shook my hand saying, "Stay true, Niki!"

Ramones guy left and I was headed to my room, when I saw Mike and Tré playing craps at a half-empty table in the dark. I stood back watching, trying to keep my mouth SHUT. Then a pit boss told me to beat it. But, I didn't want to beat it! A woman nearby saw what happened. "He's kicking you out because you're not gambling," she said.

I bought some chips.

A craps table is a *k-razy* looking thing. It's like a sunken pool table with all kinds of gibberish written on its' green felt top. I never gamble, not in casinos anyway. I had no clue what anything meant. Neither did the 10 or so other fans standing around the table grinning, trying to hold it together. On my roll, I tossed the dice so hard one bounced off the table landing on the floor.

In my moment of humiliation, Tré Cool leaned over the table, "Lemme see your tattoo."

"Me?" I asked, looking around.

"Yeah you!"

I showed him the Green Day tattoo on the inside of my left forearm.

"That is so cool!" I believe were his exact words. Tré Cool thinks *I'm* cool?!?

"That's right, Tré Cool thinks I'm cool!" I bragged to myself as I stood in line at the grocery store, the drugstore and the bank the week after I came home.

Knowing the night couldn't get any better, I tucked my special-issued Green Day chips in the pocket of my black jeans. Looking back at the table I blurted, *"Thank you for such a fucking awesome show!!"*

Oh how they laughed.

The next morning the Grammy nominations for 2004 were announced. Green Day was still at The Hard Rock. It was said Billie Joe had been strutting around wearing polka dotted boxer shorts over his pants proclaiming, "I've just been nominated for seven Grammys; I can wear whatever the fuck I want!"

On the Boardwalk in Atlantic City

Months later, in April of 2005, Green Day played Atlantic City and I was there. In case my pit survival in Las Vegas had been a fluke, I bought two tickets for the AC show: one for the pit, one for the bleachers. Inside the garish Taj Mahal Casino, I followed the people in green couture from the parking garage to the line forming outside the *inside* Mark Ettis Arena.

A group of fans behind me talked frantically. They'd gotten distracted in the parking garage and forgotten to ditch their coats. They wanted to be in the pit, badly. My experience in Las Vegas taught me that you can't bring anything into the pit unless you want to lose it.

"I couldn't help overhearing," I said, "I have an extra seat in the bleachers. You can put your coats on it. That's what I'm doing."

"What are you going to do for a seat?" one of the girls asked. I told her why I had two tickets. Giving away my seat meant I was committed to the pit. We piled our coats on it and moved to the giant dance floor.

Getting as near the stage as I could, a girl to my left was wigging out. Rummaging through her purse she cried, "Oh god, I've gotta take my anxiety medicine before the show starts!" Her friend said it was too late -- they were in the pit and there was nothing to drink anyway.

"WHAT AM I GONNA DO?!?" She freaked.

I tried engaging her in conversation. Her biggest fear: she'd never been in a pit before. I showed her how I'd been protecting myself by holding my arms at chest level, like a boxer. I warned that the crowd might begin to move as one and that she should just go with it. If all else failed, I said, signal security and get pulled out. Once the music started, the two of us were immediately separated by the first great push of the crowd.

The opening act, My Chemical Romance, was amazing. Gerard Way spoke to the young girls in the audience urging them to walk away from inappropriate sex with any of the guys attached to the bands, i.e. roadies.

"Girls, it's just a bunch of sweaty, gross guys backstage and they're probably going to try and take advantage of you. Love yourselves." It turned out to be the theme of the night. During Green Day's set, a blonde teenage fan, oblivious to Mr. Way's advice, lifted her T-shirt exposing her braless-self to the world atop some dude's shoulders. Catching a glimpse, Billie Joe covered his eyes urging, "Please don't do that!"

Shifted by the crowd, my new pit-mate was a guy with a studded dog collar around his neck and a short black Mohawk. As Green Day started one of their unique intros, Mohawk man put his arm around my shoulder and the two of us belted out the song *Maria* in tandem. Then *we* got separated!

When the show ended, I got my coat from the extra seat and headed out. Walking through the exit door, I ran into high-anxiety girl. She was all smiley. "Hey!" She called after me, "You were right! I didn't need my medicine at all. Green Day is better than drugs!!"

"Yea!" I shouted back.

It would be three months until I saw Green Day again, this time in Europe.

Welcome to Bawlmer, hon!

Oh Baltimore

Baltimore, Maryland, is a mystery. That's why I moved there from Northern Virginia in 1990. It was still a gritty, wild port of call; a place with its own rules due to lack of cops due to lack of money. I had a classic Baltimore row house in the Canton area of the city: 1105 South Curley Street. In 1995, my mom died. I took the money she'd set aside for me and bought a home in the Charm City suburb of Catonsville, Maryland.

The quaint town of Catonsville is situated 20 minutes southwest of Baltimore City proper. It's a real-life Mayberry R.F.D. with old gingerbread homes, wrap-around porches and white picket fences. Every Fourth of July, all good Catonsvillians have picnics in their backyards. At 3 p.m. everyone attends the Fourth of July parade down the main street of Frederick Road. And after the parade, everyone takes naps to rest before the fireworks later that night at Catonsville High School.

My Cottage

Baltimore is enjoying a cultural renaissance. Part of that renaissance has been the Creative Alliance; an artists' collective situated in Highlandtown, East Baltimore. The Creative Alliance was generous enough to give me a place to perform workshops of a musical I was writing, *Here Lies Dorothy Parker*. To repay them, I joined the Alliance and started attending their fund-raising galas. The theme for their 2005 annual soiree was, interestingly, *Viva Las Vegas!*

I bumped into my friend and fellow Alliance member Helen McCracken. Helen and I met in 2003 at the home of local Baltimore writer Skipper McEwan. Every year, Skipper would have an "after Christmas party" in *March*. He'd invite his former Baltimore Sun cronies to chase expensive whiskey with cheap beer while puffing on fat stogies and telling tales of days gone by.

Here Lies Dorothy Parker, 2004

At Skipper's 2005 party, Helen and I took over a solarium in the manse to gab. She confessed to her obsession with the band Cream and how she had every intention of attending their London reunion concert in a few weeks. I chimed in with my Green Day stories.

When we saw each other at *Viva Las Vegas!* a month after Skipper's party, I told her how I'd bought a $40 ticket to see Green Day...*in France.* There was only one drawback, I had no money to get there. My philosophy: if I bought the ticket, I'd find the funds. When Helen stopped laughing, she said, "I'm sending you to Europe." Two days later, my round-trip British Airways ticket arrived via e-mail.

Ticket in hand, I began planning my European vacation. I booked everything online: hotel rooms, concert tickets, all my transportation. When my First Class Eurail pass came in the mail, I pored over the schedule for hours planning how to get wherever the hell I was going.

I'd been to Europe before but never by myself. I asked travel advice from anyone who had any. The best came from Barbara, an elegant, sophisticated Baltimorean. Every once in a while, she'd hire me to sing jazz tunes at her home for cocktail parties and fancy dinners. At one affair, I was seated between a Grammy winner and a Pulitzer Prize winner. Barbara's traveling advice was for me to bring a small bag, all black clothing, (it won't show dirt), and throw in some colorful accessories to spruce things up.

Sitting in her swanky, secluded home under the vaulted ceilings, I looked down at my overalls and grey T-shirt replying, "I don't think I'm gonna need to accessorize." More importantly, she told me to get out and explore. I told her Green Day was playing at a festival in Belgium and that I wanted to go but thought I was too old. In her late sixties, Barbara looked over the top of her reading glasses, "Too old? *You're* too old? Come on now."

I drove from Baltimore to Virginia's Dulles International Airport on the 28th of June, 2005. Checking my bag, the woman behind the British Airways counter made a face when she looked at my ticket. "What is it? What's wrong?!?" I asked frantically. "Hold on just a moment," she said as she picked up the telephone. Holy shit, what the hell's wrong with my ticket? What? WHAT?!? She hung up the phone.

"It looks as though you've been upgraded to First Class!"

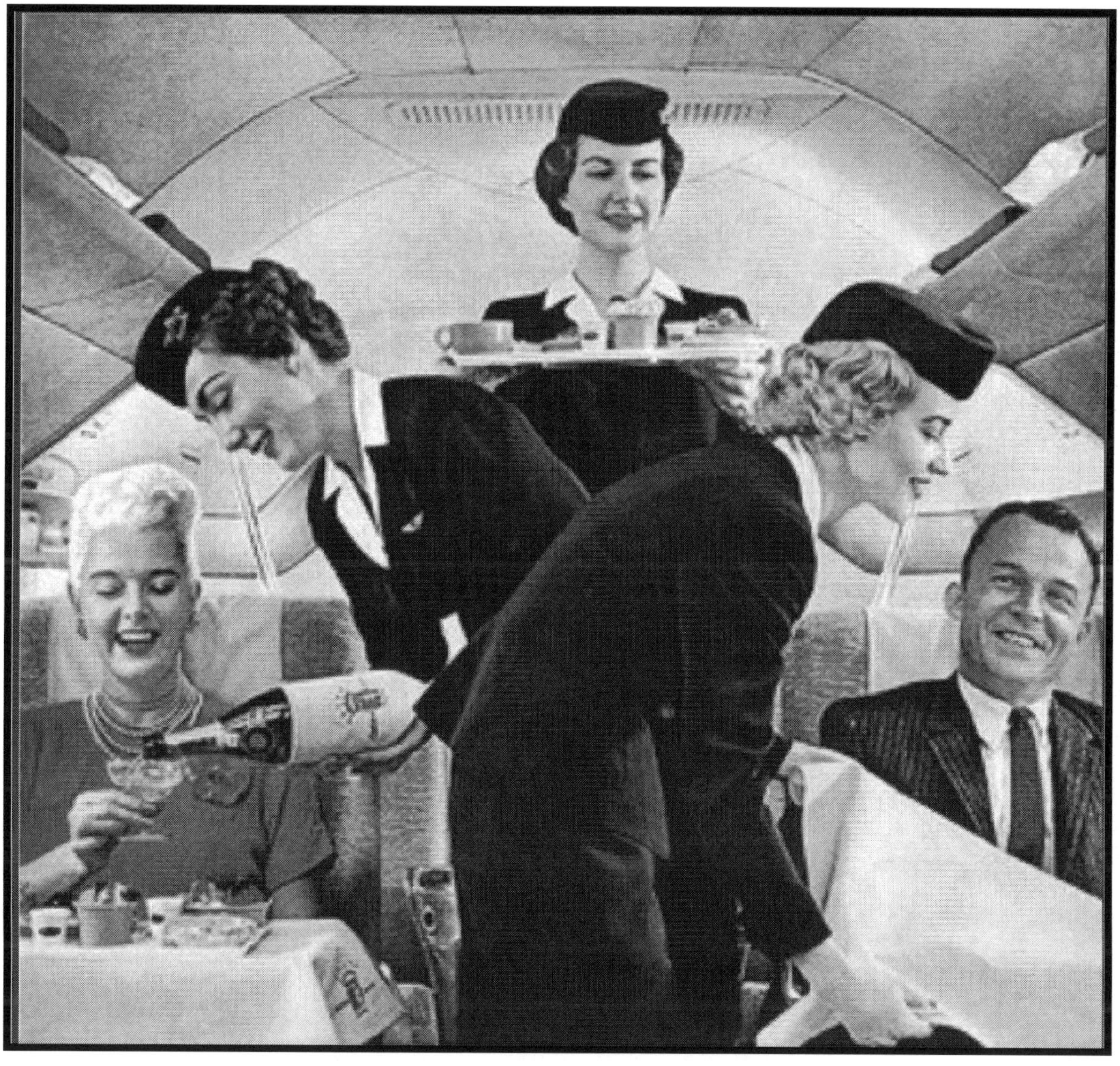

Even with lightening hitting the plane, I made it to London and spent the rest of the night at the Dawson House, or, *the tiniest bed & breakfast in the world.* The beige plastic R.V.-sized bathroom in my 6' x 8' room was so small the shower hose cleaned the whole thing: the floor, not the shower, had the only drain.

They didn't like me too much at the Dawson House. Hey, it wasn't my fault they didn't tell me how to use that weirdo phone in my room and how every time I pressed the buttons on it, it rang in the manager's office *after midnight.* It was their fault I tells ya!

Needless to say, the next morning my complimentary English Breakfast was served with a side of *scram!*

THE CHUNNEL!!

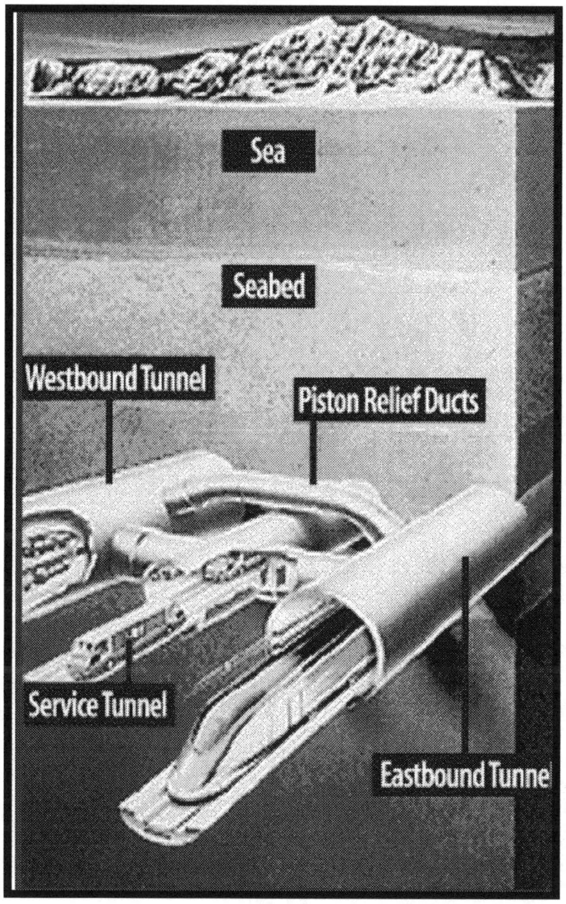
Sea
Seabed
Westbound Tunnel
Piston Relief Ducts
Service Tunnel
Eastbound Tunne

The goal for rest of my day was to cross the English Channel to get to France.

There are several options when crossing the Channel: on a boat, on a plane, in a Speedo or in *The Chunnel* -- a 26-mile underwater freak-out fest.

Agorophobes, such as myself, hate being trapped in situations that are unfamiliar and hard to escape. It's irrational, I know, because essentially, that's life.

Thank goodness for the *land* train I boarded in Paris after disembarking from the Chunnel. My new train took me to the town of Lyon, three-and-a-half-hours southeast. Green Day was playing at the city's Halle Tony Garnier the following evening.

My hotel was a block from the Saône River with its' beautiful marble bridges. I walked to the show that June 30th and saw clusters of pierced, dyed and black-clothed people walking together with purpose. I fell in line.

There was one last thing to do before entering the hall. Security is extremely tight at Green Day shows. They pat you down on the way in and they'd have confiscated my camera for sure. Slipping into one of the city's outdoor, on-the-street-pay-toilets, I hid my disposable Kodak. They may have found my Coke and they may have found my water, but they didn't find my camera.

PIT TACTICS

Needed: deep pockets and gum.

Pockets are nifty for stashing lots of things during a show like, say, drugs, phones, money, condoms. Everything must be bolted down. Also top of the list: gum. You simply must chew it!

Bouncing around and singing for over two hours conjures up a powerful thirst and in the pit there's no way to eat or drink. Once you're in, you're in. At one show I was so parched, my brain actually processed the thought, "Wring out your T-shirt and drink the sweat!" That's when I saw a woman chewing gum and thought it might help. I caught her attention by pointing to my jaw while fake chewing. That piece of Juicy Fruit saved my ass.

In Lyon, the security guards were armed with bottles of water. From their posts in front of the stage, they'd scan the crowd for anyone showing signs of dehydration. Once found, they'd point a water bottle in the person's direction and either spray them or shoot the water directly in their mouth. Mid-show, I pointed to my mouth like a baby bird chirping for food and was given a long, welcomed stream of H_2O.

Lyon a really long time ago.

Halle Tony Garnier

In 1909, the magnificent Halle Tony Garnier was built as an "industrial city" for the Universal Exhibition. Years later, part of it was transformed into a slaughterhouse. Now, it's reminiscent of an ancient church. Marveling at its' structure, I got a spring water and sat on the shiny concrete floor near the stage. Two guys sat down behind me and started speaking French. Then one of them said something in the Queen's English.

The English-speaking young man and his non-English-speaking friend had several paper-wrapped plastic straws sticking out of their pockets. Asking what was up, they explained that the straws were for stealing sips of beer out of the cups of unsuspecting passersby. I enlisted a fellow fan to take a picture of the three of us with my contraband camera.

Me, the Englishman and his friend from France
in Lyon, 2005.

Photo: Mary Kate Hannah, 2006.

We're Not Gonna Take It

Photo: Kerry Harris

GREEN DAY ENJOYS:
1. Trashing authority.
2. Doing the unexpected.
3. Getting raunchy.
4. Adoring their fans.

In France, as I'd seen in the U.S., Billie Joe engaged the audience in a call and response *Hey-Oh* which turns into an unreal Om. He initiates, you obey. Conducting the crowd, he pits one side against the other or girls against boys or whatever he wants. You're demanded to sing loud or quiet, high or low or *lonnnnggggg*.

An incorrect response could get you a full moon.

"Moon over Matika"
Photo: Kerry Harris

Then, there are the future rock stars: members of the audience picked by the band to play a song on their idols' instruments. During the *American Idiot* tour, that song was *Knowledge,* written by the band Operation Ivy. Green Day and Operation Ivy were originally both on Lookout Records. Green Day has spoken of how the ska-punk band influenced their sound.

Every show was dotted with homemade signs reading, *"I CAN PLAY KNOWLEDGE!! PICK ME!!!!!!!!!"*

Green Day selects a guitarist, a bass player and a drummer from the pit. Billie Joe asks each one if they know the song. If they lie, they receive a harsh, *"Get the fuck off my stage, you little shit!"* By the time the makeshift band finishes, the guitarist walks away with the gitbox and at least one of kids gets to do a stage dive. There's no way to avoid stage divers in the pit; you either put your arms up blindly to help catch or bend your knees and *DUCK!*

Future rock star by Jaymee Collier.

When the show in Lyon ended, 40,000 Frenchmen and I exited Halle Tony Garnier and were pummeled by a rainstorm already in progress. Traffic snarled around me as I followed the scurrying crowd into the nearest underground Metro. Dripping and matted with Green Day confetti, we stood quietly waiting for the train.

Then, from a distant tunnel, came a faint but clear *Heyyyy-Ohhhh!* We spontaneously responded: *Heyyyyyyy-Ohhhhh!!!!* smiling and laughing.

Photo: Kasia Kwiatkowska

Waffles and Mud

A First Class Eurail ticket lets a broke-ass person like me roam the continent in comfort for cheap. You purchase your train ticket based on how many days you're going to travel. First Class is light-years away from Second Class and not much more expensive. First Class also guarantees you a seat; that way you'll never have to curl up and sleep on the floor if the train is over-booked. (I've done it.) Also, First Class has embarrassingly better food that's sometimes delivered right to your seat.

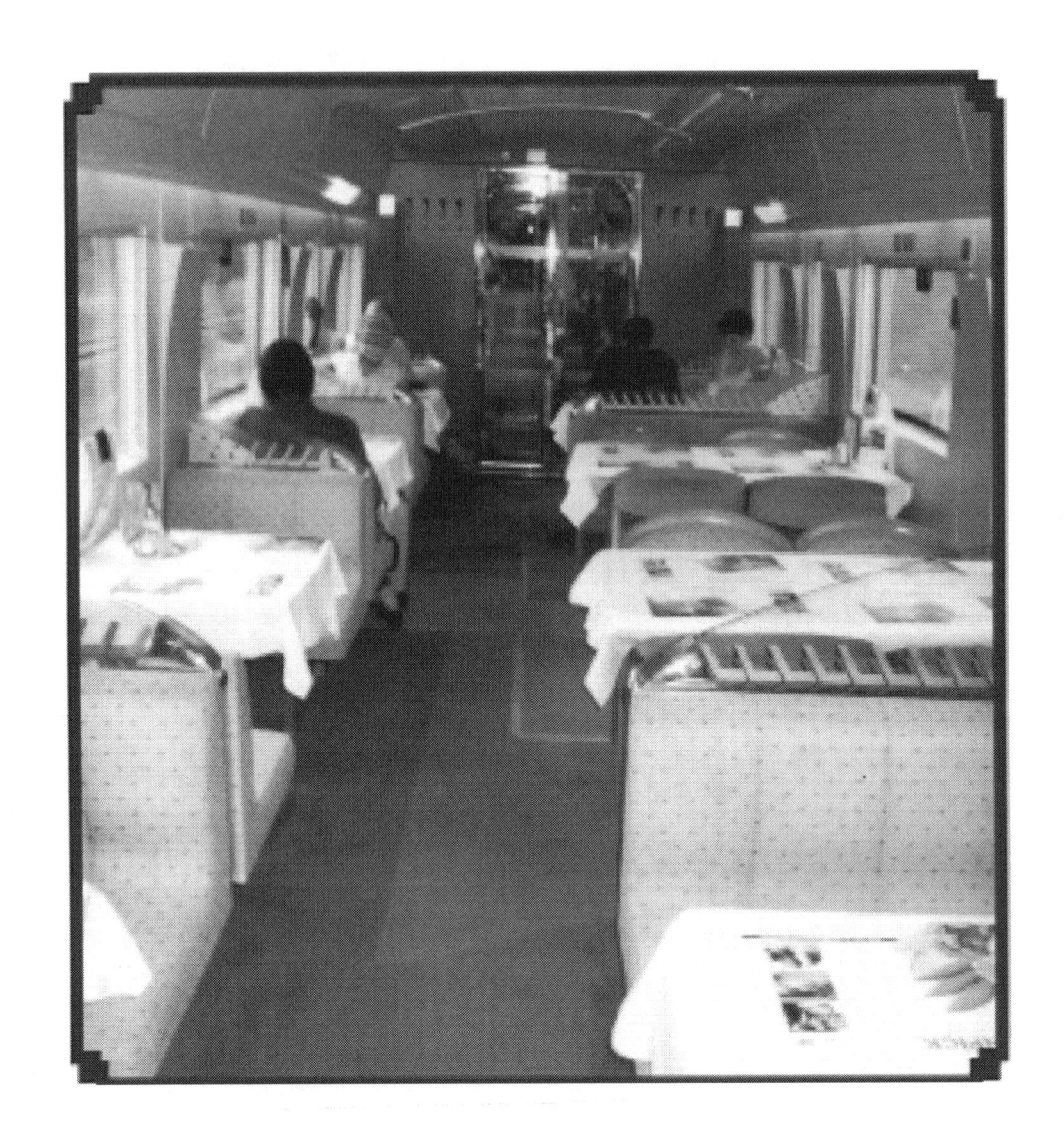

First Class dining on the way to Belgium by me.

Leuven, Belgium, June 30, 2005, by me.

The morning after the Lyon show, I boarded the First Class section of a train bound for a small town outside Brussels, Belgium: Leuven. Since 1974, the 11th century town has been home to Rock Werchter; a two-day, open-air music festival. In July 2005, a pass for the shindig included entrance to the shows, a bus ride to the location and a colorful, woven wristband.

When I arrived, the residents of the medieval town were experiencing unseasonable heat and humidity. Rain threatened to cancel the event. I got off the train and walked to the Holiday Inn Garden Court. On the way, I passed outdoor cafés jammed with diners. As I got closer to the hotel, *everyone* had handmade cones filled with luscious scoops of ice cream. I stopped in a fragrant confectionery and got one scoop of chocolate and one scoop of mint chocolate chip to fill my authentic Belgian waffle cone.

Early the next morning, I walked back to the railroad station where buses were waiting to take fans to the festival grounds. I got on one of the clunky motor carriages and was surprised at its ability to wind around Leuven's dangerously narrow streets with the ease of a slalom skier. In less than an hour, we were greeted by acres and acres of fields populated by thousands of festival goers and their tents.

Due to the rainy conditions, festival organizers went into high gear bolstering the muddy ground where concertgoers would be raging all day and night. Thousands of pounds of sand were trucked in and dumped on the mud. The sand was then covered with black rubber tiles creating a sturdy dance floor.

In Leuven, as at every show, Green Day opened with a pre-recorded overture of songs including *Oh Mickey You're So Fine, Y.M.C.A.* and the Ramone's *Blitzkrieg Bop.*

(Not my hairy arm!)

And what about the Pink Bunny! Pink Bunny is a Green Day staple. After the overture, a person in a pink bunny suit springs on stage to chug several beers. Pink Bunny's identity is top-secret. At every show, she/he gets drunk, does his/her...*dance,* then staggers off.

Green Day hit the Rock Werchter stage that night and played their asses off under a shiny disco ball.

And I danced and I danced and I danced.

Oh man was I hungry and thirsty after the show! I walked through the concession alley where I met a forlorn Canadian begging to buy my fancy woven wristband. He'd been trying to get in to see the bands for hours. Done with mine,
I carefully slid it off and received a much needed $75.

Kimberly Martin snaps
Pink Bunny chugging.

A sandwich vendor called to me from his stand, "You look hungry!" I went over to his little 'tent' where he made me a great vegetarian sub for free.

When I got back to the hotel, I threw my wet, muddy Chucks into a Leuven Holiday Inn plastic laundry bag and decided to clean them when I got home. *Twist...*

The following day, LIVE 8 was happening around the world. LIVE 8 was a series of concerts held simultaneously in the Group of Eight States: Canada, France, Germany, Italy, Japan, Russia, the United Kingdom and South Africa. There was also a concert held in Philadelphia, Pennsylvania.

From the LIVE 8 Website:

"On 2 July 2005, an estimated 3 billion people came together in the fight against extreme poverty. LIVE 8 - 10 concerts featuring over 1000 musicians from across the globe - asked people not for their money, but for their voice. The LIVE 8 Website is retained as a historical record of what happened on this amazing day and in the weeks that followed as the world's political leaders took notice."

My trip included *LIVE 8 Berlin*.

WILLKOMEN

Nazis scare me.

Hearing my first *Achtung* on the train to Germany, I almost fled. Instead, I stayed aboard for the eight hour ride to Berlin. The risk? The concert had no schedule, no time lineup for the bands. I took a chance and arrived in Berlin at 2 p.m. Even if I missed the entire LIVE 8 concert, going to Germany would still be an adventure. Now I was into the thrill.

Once in Berlin I: bounced off the train, ran to my hotel, had an anxiety attack, took a Xanax, changed my clothes, sprinted down the street, caught a cab, jogged through the groomed gardens of The Freedom Tower grounds, pushed through thousands of Germans and was finally stopped by annoyed fans having none my shenanigans.

Out of breath, I managed to rasp to the woman beside me, "Has Green Day played yet?" As the words left my mouth, actor/activist Tim Robbins took the stage and bellowed, *"All the way from Oakland, California, Green Day!"*

A pin from at the gift shop in the Hotel Berlin.

Au revoir

The London Eye Observation Wheel

On July 4th, I was back in England on my way home. Exhausted and sick, I dozed off in the park under the London Eye observation wheel. This incredible circle of engineering sits across the Thames River from Big Ben. I got up and dragged myself to Heathrow Airport. On the plane, I eased into my First Class seat, ate my First Class meal and fell asleep under my First Class blanket not waking from my dreams until we landed in America amidst the fireworks of Independence Day.

BACK IN THE U.S.A.

I crashed my purple G.M.C. Sonoma pickup truck on the way to the August 30, 2005, Green Day concert in Columbia, Maryland.

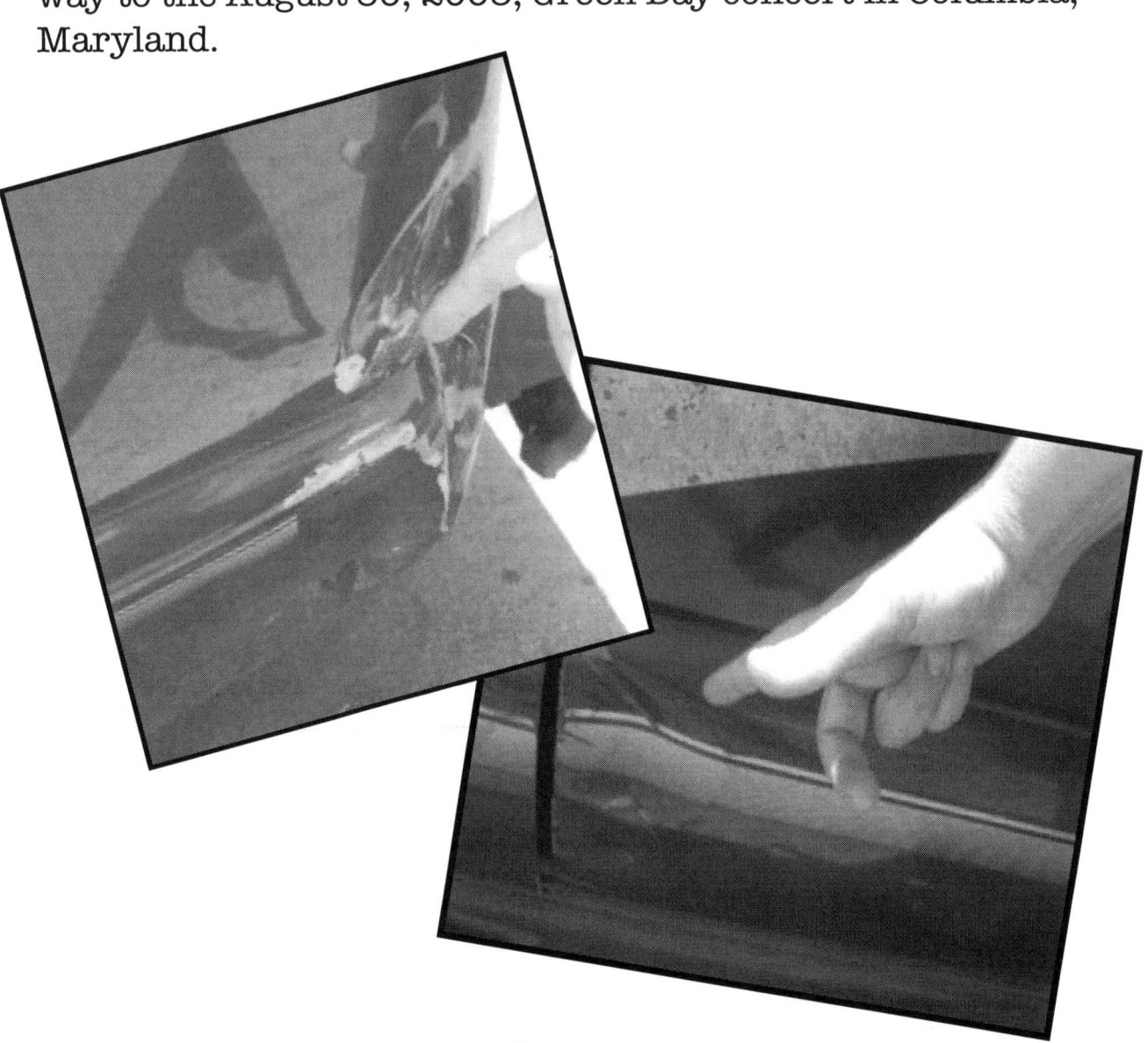

It was so stupid. I didn't leave enough time to get to Merriweather Post Pavilion. Jittery and hyper, I zoomed across 175 West driving faster than I should. That's why I didn't see the red SUV stopped in front of me until it was too late. Swerving left to avoid a wreck, I heard the distinctly creepy sound of metal on metal. The back of my truck was crunched as it sheared off the tire of a tiny rust-colored car in the left lane. The little rust car now tilted on its passenger-side rim. Making it worse, the car was full of tired looking men in dirt-covered overalls.

It turned out, the wreck wasn't just me, little rust car and red SUV. Red SUV was the *5th* in a now 7-car-pile-up. It all happened on the exit lane for the Green Day show. *Everyone was fucking up!*

The police came. The fire department came. The sun set. I was sure the concert had started. The cops let me off with a warning but I'll never forget the image of those sad, dusty men walking down the shoulder of 175 after refusing a ride from the police. No time for tears, I floored it. In seven minutes, I was running down the aisle of Merriweather, skipping over steps to the pit while listening to the opening strains of *American Idiot.*

Atlantic City Redux

It's only a three hour drive from Baltimore to Atlantic City. I took that jaunt again in May 2006 to see a tribute concert for Elvis Costello. The show, part of *VH1's Decades Rock*, featured Fiona Apple, Death Cab for Cutie and Billie Joe.

I had a cheap seat in a lame section. The afternoon of the show, I looked for a better one. Online sites I checked had lots of unsold seats and if the seats were empty at 4 p.m. I knew they'd be empty at 9 p.m. I wrote the numbers on my hand so I could find them once inside the arena. My plans were foiled as the lighting was so dim inside I couldn't see what I'd written. I spied the VH1 TV cameras and followed their aim right to the expensive blue, folding-chairs. Some very nice people saw me scrounging for a place to sit and said, "We have an empty seat if you'd like it." The two couples that offered me the seat were pals of the show's producer.

Mid-show, a rather large gentleman approached and asked my nice new friends if they wanted to go to an after-party. They said 'yes' and asked me if I wanted to come. Yes, I did. The rather large gentleman gave each of us a pink polka-dotted strip of white paper. I politely asked, "What is this?" He barked, "It's a wristband, figure it out!"

Billie Joe was the evening's closer. Tip-toeing on stage, he played the now-famous arpeggiated introduction of *Wake Me Up When September Ends*. Those six notes were greeted with the high-pitched squeal of hundreds of teenage girls. He gave them a sly smile. As he came center stage, the audience surged toward him and it wasn't just teenage girls, it was everyone. People from the bleachers filled in the aisles on the floor. People already on the floor moved closer to the stage. Security tightened. I tried moving closer but was stopped by a guard. He asked for my ticket. I was about to get busted when my nice new friends intervened saying, *"She's with us!"*

Billie Joe's set ended with Elvis Costello joining him on stage. The two sat down with acoustic guitars and, in harmony, sang Green Day's *Good Riddance* and Costello's *Alison*. Everyone sang. Billie Joe and Elvis sat back listening.

The lights came up, the crowd dissipated and my hosts and I trekked to the after-party in the Maharaja Suite on the 49th floor. Flashing my pink polka-dotted wristband at security, I climbed a spiral staircase to a second floor where there was an open bar, lavish spread of food and glamorous view of Atlantic City's glittery coast. I was expecting pretzels and beer.

These kinds of small gatherings are particularly uncomfortable for me: tiny spaces where *I know no one and no one knows me.* I couldn't stay and I couldn't go, so, I hid in the suite's fancy bathroom and started talking to myself in the mirror:

"You have to go!" Evil reflection demanded.
"I want to stay!"
"Forget it!" Evil snapped.
"But why?!?"
"Because you don't know anybody and you can't make small talk, genius."
"Fuck you!" I said, exiting my hiding place and returning to my nice new friends. I tried, really tried to chit-chat. During my effort, the expression on my face must have changed. "What is it?" one of them asked. "Oh, nothing. Would you excuse me for a second."

It was the too-close sight of Billie Joe's spritzed hair and his wife Adrienne's dreadlocks that made me rehide in the bathroom. Nearly everyone was gone by the time I came out. My nice new friends were still living it up but, it was time for me to go. I said my good-byes and walked down the spiral staircase from whence I came. At the bottom of the steps, I became disoriented and couldn't find the suite's exit. To the left was a room with a couple of couches. To the right, I smacked into one of Green Day's security guards.

"I know you," he said scanning my face.

"Yeah, I met you in Las Vegas," I said.

"I remember your face but not your name."

I told him my name and after I did, he pointed his thumb over his right shoulder saying, "It's just friends and family back there." I didn't know what the hell he was talking about. But now I was curious. I peered over his shoulder. In the darkened room behind him were Billie Joe, Adrienne and several others on a couch. Seeing my head, they looked in my direction. I hit the deck in front of the guard sputtering, "No, no! Jesus Christ! I don't want to go in there! I'm looking for the exit!" Laughing, he pointed to the way out.

Bullet in a Bible

I am not a Hobson, a Dewey, a Schley, nor a Sampson, but I was a High Private in Co. C., 8th N. Y. Cavalry, and carried this little Testament in my blouse pocket, which, in two battles, saved my life from bullets, as represented in the above photo. The bullet in the upper corner was shot at me at Cedar Creek, Va., October 19, 1864. The bullet in the centre crashed into the Testament during the battle of Appomattox (better known as Lee's surrender), April 8th and 9th, 1865.

Director Sam Bayer's Green Day documentary *Bullet in a Bible* was released in the fall of 2006. The film captures the band's performances at The Milton Keynes Bowl outside London in June 2005. In a two day punk extravaganza, Green Day performed before 65,000 of their own fans each night. It was a personal best. Bayer, who had worked with Nirvana, directed all of the *American Idiot*-era videos, most notably *American Idiot* and *Boulevard of Broken Dreams*.

On November 2, 2006, the film debuted for one night only in selected theaters across the country. I went to the multiplex monolith near my home which was very close to the crash with little rust car over a year earlier. Inside the United Artist Snowden Square Stadium 14, I was happily in a line with a bunch of parents and their teenage children. One mom and son had driven three hours from Maryland's Eastern Shore.

A grey haired dad in front of me looked burnt. "Are you a fan?" I asked.

"Not really. I can't believe I'm even here. My daughter and her friend are so nuts for this band. I don't get it. I tried to get them tickets to the Merriweather Post show, but we were too late. Then I tried taking them to a show in the Midwest, but we couldn't make that happen either." He sighed, "You have *no* idea!"

"Actually, I do." The teenage girls giggled as I flashed my Green Day tattoo.

"*Wow!*" They sang.

"Have you seen them live?" I asked.

"*No!*" They cried.

As the line moved, Dad walked slightly ahead while the girls stayed back with me. Making sure no one could hear her, his daughter whispered, "We *did* see them! We snuck out and saw them at Merriweather. Don't tell my dad."

"Don't worry, your delinquency is safe with me," I said as we walked into the theater.

Let's go back: back to the back of the rack. On January 7, 2005, Billie Joe gave an interview at the City University of New York. *Walking Contradiction* was part of The New York Times' *Time's Talks* series. Three interviews were taking place in the same building at the same time that night; one with Bill Murray, one with Susan Sarandon and one with Billie Joe.

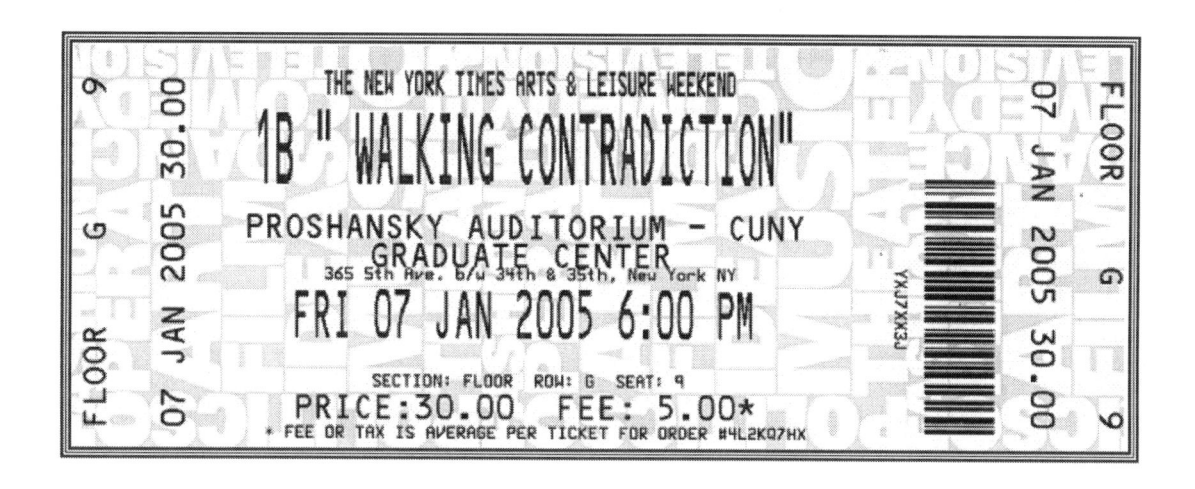

The interviews were being filmed. Camera operators and frantic production assistants buzzed everywhere. When the lights went down and Billie Joe walked on stage, every person jumped out of their seat. I thought the audience was going to eat him alive. The hysteria settled and New York Times music critic Jon Pareles spoke with Billie Joe about his life, his music and his influences.

At the end of the chat, Pareles announced a question and answer period. I sprang from my seat in the middle of Row G. In two giant *Mother-May-I* steps, I landed in line only a few people behind the microphone.

The thing is...*I had no question!* Standing in fear, I could feel heavy breathing behind me. It was coming from an over-six-foot-tall young man having a melt down.

"What's wrong?" I asked as the line to the microphone grew ever shorter.

"I think I'm gonna faint! I mean look, *it's Billie Joe! He's right there!*" He panted. "I think I'm gonna pass out!" I told him to breathe in through his nose and out through his mouth as I desperately thought of a question. What did I want to know? By the time I reached the mic, I'd figured it out.

When I first heard *American Idiot*, the songs that hit me hardest were the title tune and *Wake Me Up When September Ends*. At the time, I told a friend *Wake Me Up When September Ends* was one of the greatest songs I'd ever heard. She qualified my statement replying, "Best *'rock'* song." "No. *Any* song," I said.

Reaching the mic, I asked Billie Joe if he'd sing a little of the ballad. As I asked, the crowd burst at its' seams shouting out Green Day song requests, some I'd never heard before. *"1000 Hours!" "Look for Love!"*

Billie Joe chuckled, "*Look for Love.*" *Look for Love* is the first song he ever recorded...at five-years-old. I hadn't anticipated all the screams from the audience and tried to concentrate. Billie Joe stared at me quizzically, "Sing something?!?" I wasn't sure what to do; the audience, the hot lights, the mic in my face; my mind was short circuiting.

"Yeah," I laughed nervously, "just sing *something!*" The crowd went nuts again. Billie Joe was noticeably distressed. It was weird. Regaining my composure, I joked that I'd even like to hear one of the show tunes he'd sung for hospital patients when he was a kid. With trepidation, he started singing the show tune *Chicago* then stopped abruptly. "Oh my god, if I had a guitar I would but..."

I thanked Billie Joe and turned to walk to my seat. Apparently, he wasn't done. "Oh God, man, that is so nerve-wracking to try to do that!" I felt shitty. It hadn't occurred to me that *he* might be nervous. The crowd quieted. I didn't know how to respond but I knew I wanted to hear him sing, so I repeated, in a high voice, "Well, I was thinking of a little bit of *Wake Me Up When September Ends*, maybe a capella."

He shuffled a bit and sang the first few lines of the song with great vulnerability. Everyone cheered. I felt horrible.

Slumping into my seat, the woman next to me patted my arm, "Great question!" I didn't think so; I'd been pushy and insensitive. I felt like a jackass. A big, loud-mouthed, jackass.

Later, standing in the meet-and-greet line smushed between two 30-something sisters who knitted color-coordinated scarves for the whole band and a greasy-faced 13-year-old boy dying to put his paws all over my Special Edition *American Idiot* hardback booklet, I plunged into anxiety: "God that was bad. Maybe I should get the hell out of this line."

Billie Joe smiled and talked to fans as he signed autograph after autograph. A woman behind me sighed, "That poor man," looking at the 300 people waiting to get his signature. When I reached the table where Billie Joe was sitting, his face fell. *Holy shit, I knew I should have gotten out of this line!* Then he said, "I'm really sorry about that singing thing."

Shocked and thankful he wasn't pissed, I said, "That's OK."

Getting autographs is not my thing. When I was a kid, I'd get them for my mother at summer-stock productions. She was shy and I didn't mind. Now, here I was for the first time with my own open booklet. Billie Joe scribbled his name on it as I said, "I saw you guys in Las Vegas." I extended my hand and he shook it with a kind and weary smile.

Fill in any cliché about meeting a hero:
I couldn't move-
I couldn't breathe-
Time slowed to a crawl-
Time rushed by-
I'll never wash this hand again!

Scratch that last one. After all, I was in Manhattan, isle of bacteria. The hand had to be washed.

Death and Resurrection

American Idiot upended my life so exquisitely that after years of fear I was free. I learned how to have fun by myself and with others, how to fly without panic and how to infuse my own music and life with spirit and guts.

Great art has no boundaries. *American Idiot* is great art and I'm glad I got to catch that monster wave right along with the band, riding it out until the last crash landed on my middle-aged shoreline.

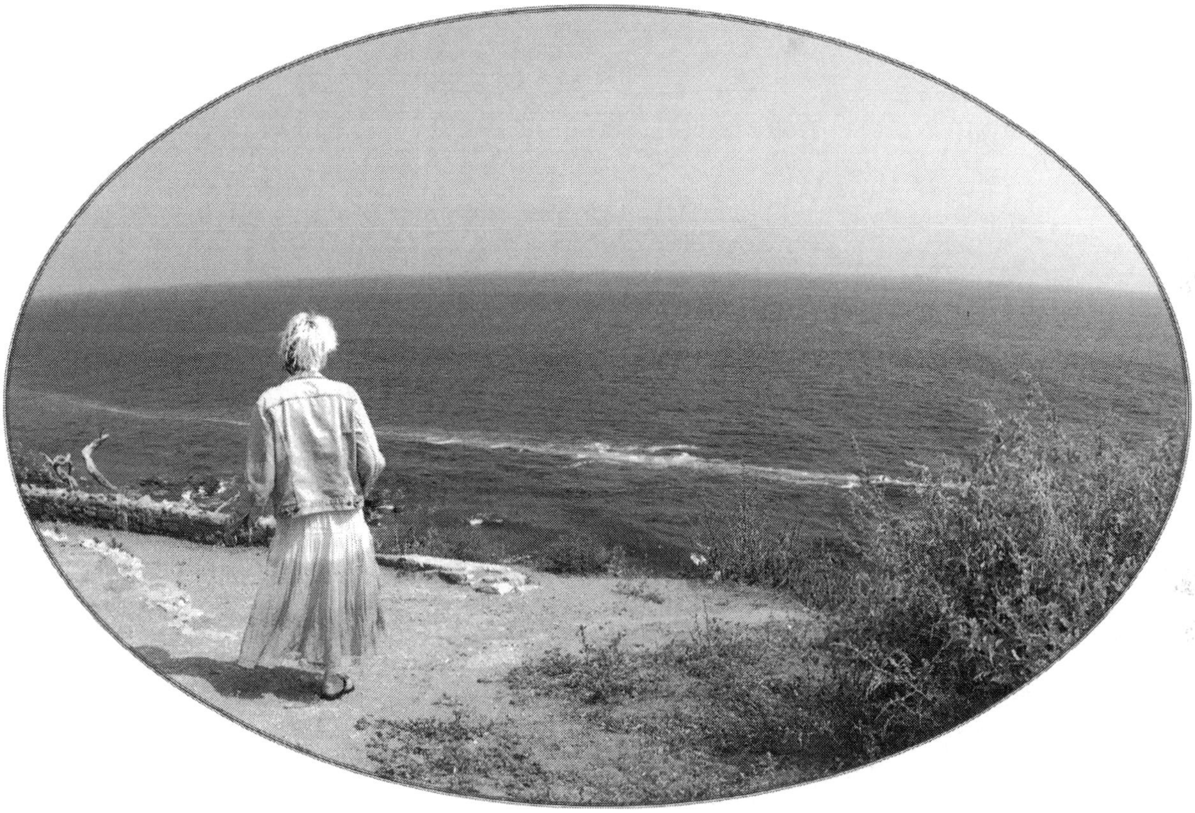

Photo: Cheryl Groff

Photographers:

Jaymee Collier--Ottawa, Canada

Jimmy Douglas--Clark, NJ
http://www.flickr.com/photos/futuredaydreamphotography/

Eleonora *Eliu* Gatti--Milan, Italy

Toni Ann Graffigna--Staten Island, New York

Katie "McPansy" Grogan--Kansas City, Kansas

Kerry Harris--Adelaide, Australia

Rita Heise--Palmyra, New Jersey

Kasia Kwiatkowska--Norway

Naomi Lir--Toronto, Canada

Kimberly Martin--High Bridge, New Jersey

Oscar Muñoz--Bogota, Colombia
http://www.oscarmm.com/

Eileen Pretzel--The Bronx, New York City

Mary Rosenblatt--Cromwell, Connecticut

Dorie Watts--Springboro, Ohio

Beth Wieman--St. Charles, Missouri

Illustrations by Alex Langenstein

Alex Langenstein lives in Bellevue, Washington.
She graduated from the Vancouver Institute of Media Arts
in Vancouver, B.C., Canada, with specialties in both
2-D and 3-D animation. An accomplished
illustrator, painter and animator.

Photo: Eleonora Gatti

How Seize the Green Day Landed in the Rock and Roll Hall of Fame

In 2013, I donated a rare recording to the Rock and Roll Hall of Fame. I discovered it in my Catonsville garage in 2001. Singing on the unmarked cassette was my late friend, the great Eva Cassidy. She was performing with Mick Fleetwood of Fleetwood Mac and members of her band. To this day, no one knows how I ended up with tape including me. Well, except for the fact that I was married to Eva's piano player at the time.

Five years after Eva died, I found a moldy briefcase in my garage and discovered several cassettes with no labels. I listened to each one. When I heard Eva, I stopped. What the hell? I played the tape once then had it digitized making copies for myself.

Eva was extraordinary. She was giving. She excelled in visual arts and her musical ability was astounding. However, despite her gifts, she had no belief in her vast talent. It wasn't her fault. She never got the support she needed. The damage was fatal.

A year before she died, she told me she was destined not to have a career in music. I told her she was wrong. Still, she was unknown at the time of her death from melanoma in 1996. She was only 33.

I met Eva in the late 1980s. Her then-boyfriend owned a recording studio and enlisted my husband to accompany her. The three of them started a band and for the next few years, they played around the Baltimore/Washington area even though she hated performing.

Eva placed this on my seat before her famous *Live at Blues Alley* performance, January, 1996. Her inability to spell was endearing.

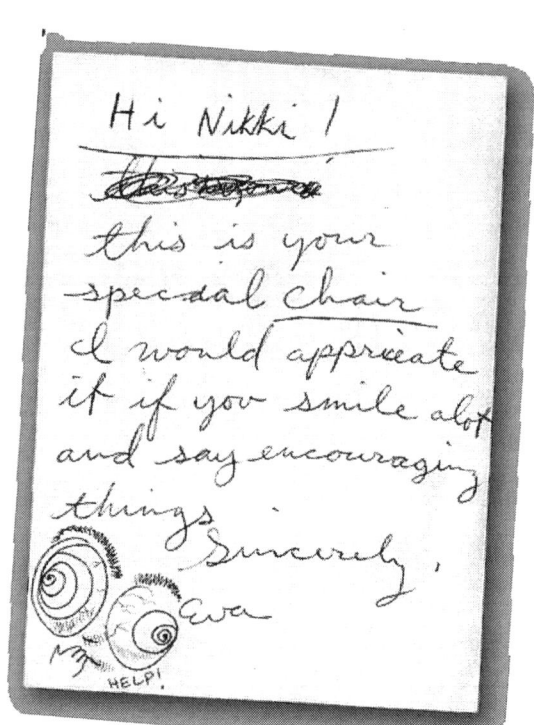

The recording was made in the early 90s. It was from a night she played Fleetwoods: a club in Virginia that somehow had a connection to Mick Fleetwood. I was never sure of the famous drummer's involvement with the place, but he would hang around and sit in with bands he liked. He really liked Eva.

For the last 14 years, Eva's estate and record company have prohibited me from releasing the recording. Both parties refuse to make it public and have never even asked to listen to it. Frustrated, I called the Rock and Roll Hall of Fame and asked if I could donate the tape for historic purposes. They were thrilled. The donation was handled by Hall of Fame archivist Anastasia Karel. However, the letter of thanks she sent me was purposefully destroyed it in 2014. I called Anastasia to ask if it could be replaced. She said 'of course.' As we were winding up our conversation about the letter, she asked,

"Hey, are you the same Niki Lee who wrote a book about Green Day?"

"Y-e-s," I answered, slowly.

"We'd like a copy for our library!"

Then I sat down...very s-l-o-w-l-y.

There you go.

That is how *Seize the Green Day* got into the Rock and Roll Hall of Fame. Thank you Anastasia. Thank you Eva. Thank you Green Day. Love~Niki

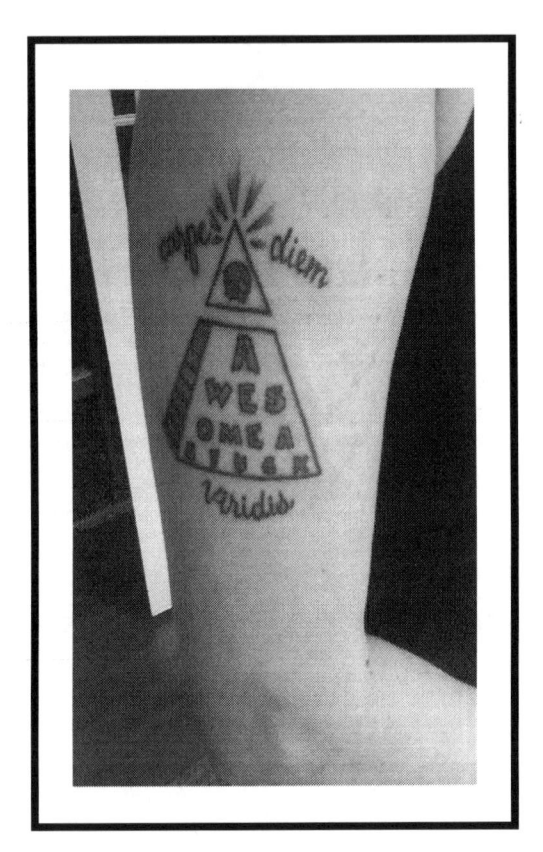

The following stories, photos and artwork were submitted by the international Green Day community in celebration of the band's induction into the Rock and Roll Hall of Fame.

Pre-Induction
Artwork: Desensitized Brat

Eileen Pretzel

"On July 29, 2013, the film *Broadway Idiot* was screened at Lincoln Center in New York City. Tickets went on sale a few weeks earlier...at midnight!

The documentary is about Billie Joe Armstrong's Broadway debut in *American Idiot*. At the screening, the woman introducing *Broadway Idiot* mentioned that she didn't know how 'you people, (us *Idiot* Green Day fans who filled up the theater), managed to buy up the tickets practically before they went on sale!'

During a Q & A with the producers and director after the screening, I stood up and said, 'I don't know if you and Green Day realize how many genuine friendships were formed because of this play, [*American idiot*], and this band. There are at least 50 people in this audience right now who are all friends.'

I was in the second row. Unbeknownst to me, all these people behind me started waving their hands in the air because they were the people I was talking about.

I added, 'That's how the tickets sold out so quickly. We, as friends, work together to make sure everyone who wants to go can. Some people aren't able to get online at midnight. So those who are able, buy lots of extras and we sort it out later!' They were floored."

Billie Joe and Eileen Pretzel on the set of *Geezer*.
New York, 2014.

Jordan Delatte and Billie Joe

"This is me and Billie Joe outside the St. James Theater the day after I went to see *American Idiot* for my 14th birthday. It was my first trip to New York City. I went with my mom and grandma. Now, I get to go to the simulcast of Green Day's Rock and Roll Hall of Fame induction. The strangest part is even though I've seen the musical and I'm going to the induction...I still haven't seen Green Day live!"

Giulia Ricciotti

"Hi guys! I'm one of your biggest fans, Giulia, from Turin, Italy. People ask me, 'Why are Green Day so important to you?' I answer, 'Every word and chord in their music makes me feel alive. It's like jumping on an emotional train and never getting off. It's not only a passion, it goes in the deepest part of my heart and it will never stop. I can't imagine my life without their music, they are an essential part of me.'

November 12, 2009, was my first Green Day show. The date will remain carved in my heart. Then, in September 2010, I traveled to the United States from Italy to retrace Green Day's history. I first visited the San Francisco Bay-area: Gilman Street, Studio 880, Rudy's Can't Fail Cafe. Then, I went to New York City to see *American Idiot* on Broadway.

I've seen you guys in Paris, Milan, Trieste, Rome, Bologna and Nimes. My dream is to come up on stage and hug each one of you! I can't wait to see you again live around the world. With all the love I have, your BIG fan Giulia, from Turin, Italy."

Giulia!

Giulia and Prima Donna.

Milena Cieślak

"One of my bucket-list goals was, 'See your favorite band as a kid in a really big arena or stadium.' I decided to realize that on my birthday. I flew to London to celebrate and to see Green Day at Emirates Stadium in England.

A day before the concert, my friends and I were walking around Soho in London. As we waited in a line for coffee, I wondered if Green Day had already arrived in town. At the exact minute we were talking about Green Day, we saw Mike Dirnt just in front of us! He was kinda surprised that I recognized him and we started a conversation.

We had a really nice chat about nothing and everything all at once and I even got early birthday wishes. He was astonished when we said we flew all the way from Poland to see the gig. He gave us a little tip to show up early at the venue if we wanted to have a good spot. Before he left, he asked us if we wanted a photo with him. I said, 'Ok. If you really want a picture with us it's no problem, man!' Then we all had a laugh attack.

And that's it. My coffee had gone totally cold, but, this is the photo!

After many hours of waiting for the concert, we made it to the exact middle of the first row. We had 60,000 people behind us with all our hearts and souls singing every single song from the top of our lungs.

I have now been to three Green Day concerts and the London show was definitely the craziest. Thanks to Mike, it was absolutely the most special one. Of course, on my bucket-list I'd written, 'It would be cool to meet Mike some day.' I can proudly check off two items."

Milena Cieślak with Mike in London, 2013.

Alyssa and Billie Joe.

Alyssa Kisel

"This photo was taken on February 21, 2011, in New York City. I was living in Atlanta, Georgia, at the time and drove to Manhattan to see Billie Joe on Broadway in *American Idiot*. I met up with two of my friends there. They kept teasing me saying, 'Maybe you'll see Billie Joe in the city.'

Not long after she said that, my friend saw him walk by. I thought she had to be kidding. I decided to look back anyway and I instantly knew the man walking away was him. It all happened so fast after that. Suddenly, I was at his side saying God-knows-what. I don't remember most of it. I thought he was ignoring me until I realized he had on headphones and couldn't hear me! He paused his Ipod and said, 'Wait, what did you say?'

We spoke briefly and I realized I wanted a picture with my idol before the moment was over. I was shaking and couldn't seem to unlock my phone. My friend was already standing by, camera in hand. He asked her if she got the picture and then I let him go on his way. It couldn't have been more perfect and is still the best day of my life."

Billie Joe and Polly Cantle, New York City, 2010.

Polly Cantle with Green Day in Berlin, August 2012.
Photo: Milena Cieślak

Drawings: ((A Joe))

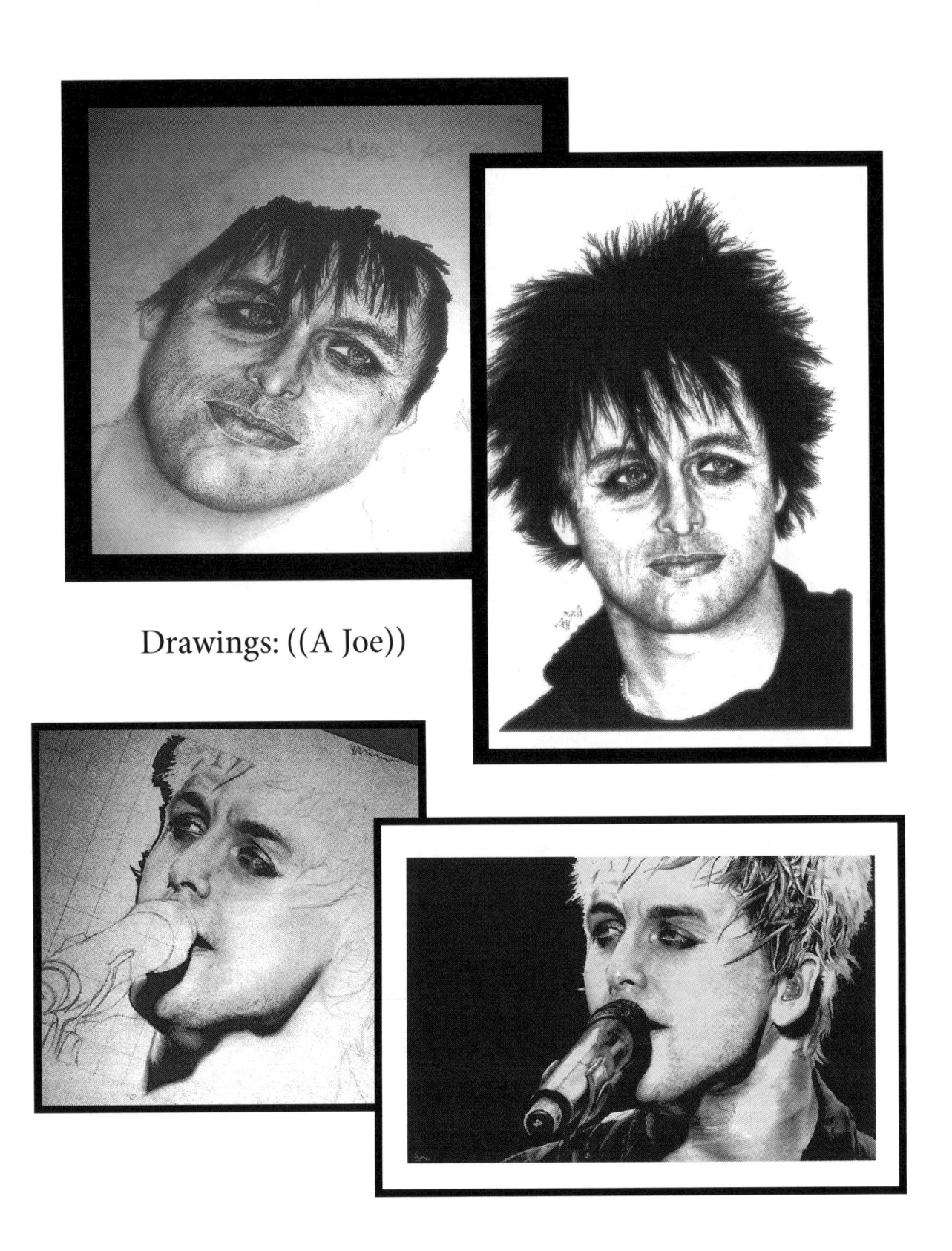

Sarah Lemke and Billie Joe, Lollapolooza, Chicago, 2010.

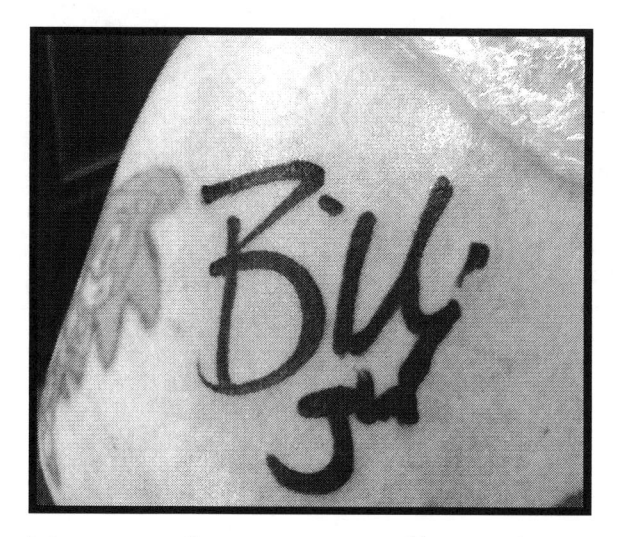

Teresa Robinson got Billie Joe's autograph during *American Idiot* on Broadway. Then she rushed to a Manhattan tattoo shop to get inked.

Sofia's ankle

Sofia Giannini

"I've been listening to Green Day since I was 12. The band made me who I am today. Thanks to them I've met so many nice people. They have made me cry tears of happiness and sadness, too. I've listened to all their albums and their parallel bands - each of them unique. I hope they keep growing because I'll be listening to them until the day I die. I love them with my life."

Stasia

"I am a Green Day fan: a fact that I have possibly denied since circa 1994 when a guy asked me what kind of music I liked. It was then I learned that Green Day was the wrong answer. This incident predates my discovery of Bob Dylan, the Beatles and the Clash. But, I remember it so well that I didn't give the band my full attention. I may have bought *American Idiot*, but more because I thought I should. It was my sister who suggested it -- usually it's the other way around.

I moved to Berkeley in 2008 and I learned about Green Day's roots in the area. I considered giving them another chance. In early April 2009, I heard about several surprise club shows the band was playing in San Francisco. I got so excited, especially after receiving an email about a show on April 14th at the Fox Theatre in Oakland. After all, one of the best places to see a band is on their home turf. I got a great seat -- second row balcony -- and was impressed by the show's production. They played all of [their new album] *21st Century Breakdown*. There was even a special free program including all the lyrics to the album.

Hearing new music before its released is one of those unique opportunities I look for from *rock'n'roll*. My initial reaction was, 'Wow, this is pretty good!' Now that I've heard it a few more times, my review is five stars! Some songs are ageless, as if I've known them my whole life. During the show, I heard someone say the band was going to play the next night at a club called the Uptown, right across the street from the Fox.

Photos by Stasia

Sure enough, I checked the Website. The show was $20 cash at door.

The next night, when I got to the Fox, the line stretched more than halfway around the block. The capacity was 575 which meant maybe 300 could comfortably fit by the stage. I was about number 335 when I reached the door. Unless I wanted to force my way through the crowd, there was no way I could see the stage. Instead, I went up to the mezzanine. But I couldn't see from there either! I saw a large screen in another room that showed the stage. That was going to have to be good enough.

The band didn't begin until 10:30 p.m., much later than the previous night. By then I was so tired I could barely stand up. I moved from the mezzanine to a bit of wall space by the front door and watched the show from there. Unfortunately, the sound had to travel through a wall before it got to me which made it muddy at best. Still, the thrill was simply getting into the club. After an hour, I left. That's when I discovered that the sound was better *outside*.

Now I can declare 'I am a fan!' -- especially after hearing Green Day perform their older songs, like the ones' from *Dookie*. Those tunes take me right back to that teenage place I've never seemed to drop."

Green Day at the Fox Theater by Stasia.

Lidia Marini

"Hi I'm Lidia from Italy and I'm 20. This photo is from a Green Day show in Bologna on June 6, 2013. It was the first time I had the opportunity to see the band and it was amazing. It was a present from my friends in the photo. Just to say, we are an Italian punk-rock/independent band called Booze Toxic."

Lydia Marini with Vincent and Sonny.

Mary of Suburbia and Billie Joe.

Mary of Suburbia

"I discovered Green Day in 2005 and fell in love! I fell in love with the music and collected all of the albums. Then, I fell in love with the band, especially Billie Joe as the person who wrote all those amazing songs and sings them with such passion. Id' heard stories of other fans meeting him. After that, I hoped to meet him, too. It happened on October 6, 2014, at the Mill Valley Film Festival in San Rafael, California. A few of my friends and I attended the premiere of the film *Like Sunday, Like Rain*. Billie Joe had a small but intense role in the movie. It was touching and made me cry. After the film, there was a question and answer period with its' director, producer and actors. Billie Joe joked about what he said when director Frank Whaley asked him to play a shitty boyfriend. His response, 'I can do that!'

The ticket included an after-party at the Tiburon Tavern. Billie Joe and his wife Adrienne were there along with other actors and the director. We saw him sitting on a sofa, surrounded by furniture and a security guard. We headed over there anyway. One of my friends got close to Billie Joe. I was wondering how to get around the furniture. The security guard saw me and told me to leave. Then Billie Joe noticed my predicament. He smiled and gestured for me to join him, moving a chair out of the way. I got nervous. I could hear my friend telling him about a band she was starting. After she finished, I gave him a hug and asked him if we could take photos. He said, 'Sure!' I took one of him and my friend. Then she took one of me and Billie Joe. He and I looked at the photo and he said, 'It's beautiful!' It was so sweet. A few minutes later he was in another part of the tavern where a birthday cake came out for Adrienne and he sang *Happy Birthday* to her. Then we left. The event may have been over but meeting Billie Joe left me with a sublime memory."

Photo:
Mary of Suburbia

Megan Pandabear-Hawks

"Me holding a guitar pick I scored after seeing the *American Idiot* touring production in San Francisco. I was second row thanks to my big sister and friend, Stephanie. She got the tickets for my birthday a couple of years ago."

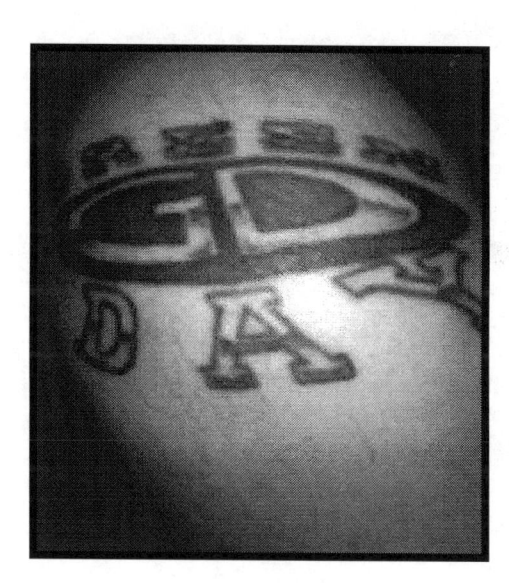

Jeff Ornstein's tattoo.

Flavia Slick and Billie Joe,
Fiera Rho, Milan, Italy, May 24, 2013.

From left: Samantha Le Sommer, Taylor Mackin, Lizzie Havok & Clare McCartan.

From left: Clare McCartan, Mike Dirnt, Lizzie Havok, Samantha Le Sommer and Taylor Mackin.

Arianna Baragiola

"My sister Camilla and I have been listening to Green Day for a very long time. They inspired us to play and compose music. We got to meet the band in 2013 when we went to see Prima Donna in Milan, Italy. Green Day was playing two days after Prima Donna. So, we went to see them, too. We spent time with them and even talked to them. When Prima Donna finished their set, Green Day decided to play a secret show for the people in the small venue. It was great!"

Arianna and Camilla

Arianna and Camilla Baragiola with Tré Cool...

...and Jason White...

...and, Billie Joe.

Vicky Sabbath Armstrong

"I went to Paris, 1000 miles from my home near Cannes, to see Green Day during their *21st Century Breakdown* tour. This picture was taken by my mom in front of the venue where we waited from 7:00 a.m. to 7:30 p.m. I played hooky to be there.

It was my first Green Day concert and I was 17. I met the fans in this photo standing on line. They talked about a banner they made they were going to hold up during the song *Hitchin' A Ride*. I said, 'It's *I want to hitch a ride!* There's a mistake!' We laughed. I've seen Green Day three times. I hope to meet Billie Joe and explain how much I worked at school to translate his lyrics to improve my English. When I was 11, I thought my efforts will pay off and one day I'll be able to tell him how much he helped me: my spiritual father."

From far right: Sabrina Alnawi, Vicky Sabbath Armstrong and Marion Cousin.

Isabel Calderón and Billie Joe.

Isabel Calderón

"I'm Isabel Calderón from Costa Rica and I've been a fan of Green Day since *American Idiot* came out. I owe that band the best day of my life. This picture was taken on October 29th, 2010, at Green Day's gig in Costa Rica. I got the chance to be called on stage and sing with Billie Joe during *Are We the Waiting*. At the end of the song, Billie Joe gave me a kiss!

On February 19th, 2011, one of my best friends Paula and I took a trip to New York City to see *American Idiot* on Broadway. Billie Joe was starring as *St. Jimmy*. The musical was perfect! In spite of the cold and our lack of understanding English, we waited for Billie Joe after the show. We wanted to tell him how grateful we were to him for everything Green Day. I even took a picture with my hero and got to exchange words with him. Those days I will never forget."

Chris Grebinski-Policicchio

"I have an auto immune disease called Alopecia. It tricks the body into thinking hair is the 'enemy' kicking it out. I went through hell growing up and spiraled into a very dark place until I found my light: music. Twenty years ago, Green Day's music was one of the few things that helped me find strength to be myself. I met Billie Joe in person a few years ago and was able to thank him. To see them inducted in the Rock and Roll Hall of Fame!?! Full circle."

Chris and Billie Joe outside the St. James Theater.

David Luis

"I decided to fly from my home in South America to New York City to see the *American Idiot* musical staring Billie Joe Armstrong. My goal? To give to Billie Joe a CD of Karratapunk: my friend's Spanish Green Day cover band. My friend, Alonso, tried to do that himself when Green Day came to Colombia for the first time on October 10, 2010. He didn't get to give them a CD, but, he *was* lucky enough to get pulled on stage to sing *Longview*. He sang amazingly and Billie Joe gave him a guitar.

On February 23, 2011, I brought four of Alonso's CDs to *American Idiot* on Broadway. At the end of the show, I ran downstairs to wait for all the actors to leave. I gave three CDs to actors in the show asking them if they wouldn't mind showing them to Billie Joe.

When Billie Joe finally appeared, people went nuts. He started signing things and taking pictures with fans. I was one of the last ones to chat with him. I gave him the CD and he started signing it. But I yelled, 'No man! That's for you!' He looked at the CD, then at me and said, 'Thanks!' He then got into a car and was whisked away. I was in ecstasy having had a guy I so admired right in front of me."

Karratapunk: https://www.facebook.com/karratapunk
Youtube channel: https://www.youtube.com/user/greatdays90

Billie Joe signing Alonso's CD.

Collage by Sabrina Scarcella.

Billie Joe and Robin Ross.

Robin Ross

"During the run of *American Idiot* on Broadway, Green Day's fan site *Idiot Nation* announced it was giving away four front row seats to the play. My friend was coming to New York for my birthday so I asked her if she'd like to see the show from the front row. She said 'yes' and I bought us tickets. A month later, it was announced that Billie Joe would be starring in the show for two months as *St. Jimmy*. His first show was right before my birthday. Not only was I in the front row, but now Billie Joe was going to be in it! A matinee was announced. I decided to go early and see if we could meet him. We waited and it paid off. I asked him to wish me happy birthday...and he did! I even got it on video. Seeing the show from front row and having my favorite rockstar wish me happy birthday made that day one of the best of my life."

Gillie Cool Carter

"There are about 30,000 stitches in this piece: stitched with love for the band I adore. The image comes from the band's *American Idiot*-era. I've been a fan since *Dookie*, but *American Idiot* saved my life. Hearing *Jesus of Suburbia* stopped me from taking a whole bottle of anxiety pills. Now I understand that I'm the way I'm supposed to be."

Cross stich by Gillie Cool Carter.

Photo: Giulia Ricciotti

Top row left to right: Anne Solek, Cheryl McCloskey, Beth Wieman and Marlene Fitzsimmons. Kneeling: Chrisoula Foofighter. Outside the St. James in New York. City.

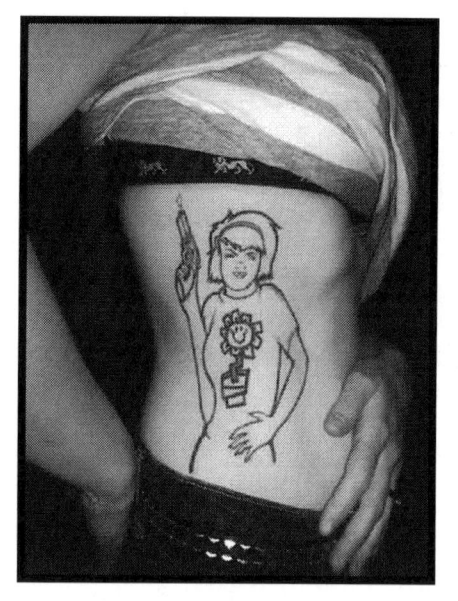

Karen Barker

Tats:
Beffy Wieman, Cheryl McCloskey and Marlene Fitzsimmons.

Lorenzo Lacarra
Bari, Italy

"In 2006, I lost my motivation in life after my grandmother died. She was everything to me. When I wasn't able to move on, Green Day's music, specifically *Jesus of Suburbia*, took my hand and guided me on my own road helping me become a real man."

Lorenzo Lacarra's tattoo before and after.

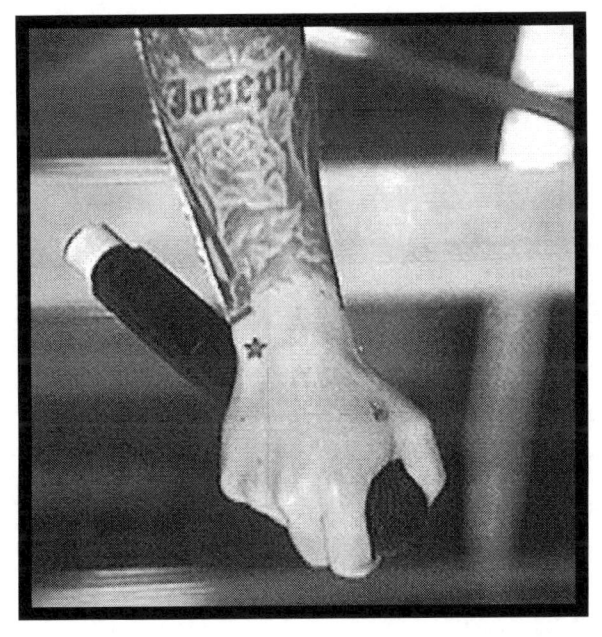

Kate-Lyn Szychoski, New Jersey
"I don't have any tattoos, I didn't get to go to the induction and I've never gotten close enough to get a *close up*! Here's a shot from a big screen at a show. I'm just happy to have seen them live."

Terilyn Rea

"I've been a Green Day fan for nearly my entire life. The first song I heard was *When I Come Around*. It played on the radio sometime in 1999 and I fell in love. But, it wasn't until the release of *American Idiot* that I became a crazy super-fan. I could relate to songs differently than when I was younger. In 2009, I convinced my mom to take me to my first Green Day concert. I remember how excited I was driving to the show. I sang through the entire Green Day discography during our trip and cried in the hotel before the shuttle even drove us to the venue in Detroit.

In 2011, I went to New York to see *American Idiot* on Broadway. I thought it was an impossible dream to see Billie Joe during his run, but then, my mom showed me a news item:

'Billie Joe Armstrong to Join Idiot for 50 shows.'

Instant heart attack. And, my mom was willing to go.

I couldn't believe it. Plus, my cousin had connections with cast member Alysha Umphress and after the show, we were allowed to go backstage and explore. Mind-blowing.

Eventually, I asked if Billie Joe was going to say 'hi' and chat. Alysha explained how he usually didn't do that so I dropped any expectations of meeting him.

Not five minutes later, there he was. I was in shock. I caught his attention by waving enthusiastically and he sassily smiled and waved back walking toward us. All I could think was, 'OH MY GOD! I LET MY GUARD DOWN! WHAT HAVE I DONE? I AM NOT PREPARED.' I kinda just stared at him. My mom came to the rescue saying everything I wanted to say and more, like, 'She has been a fan of Green Day for so long. She can play all of your songs on the guitar. We flew in from Chicago just to see you.' (She is the best human.) Billie gushed at her story and hugged me really hard then kissed me on my cheek.

After pictures and autographs, he went to visit other people, but before that he *kissed me again!* Even my mom was impressed by how down-to-earth he was and how kind he was to stop, listen and appreciate a true fan like me. That was easily the best day of my life."

Terilyn Rea and Billie Joe.

Alberto Gonzalez

"On July 22, 2009 I stumbled upon the Green Day Website and *bam!* I saw they were playing their last show of their *21st Century Breakdown* tour on August 25th in Los Angeles. My father gave me permission to go right away, but my mother had second thoughts. My father sold her on the idea.

On August 5th, the ticket was in my hand. I was shaking when I got it and was so excited that I wanted to sleep with it. Listening to Green Day albums every day annoyed my sister a lot, but I didn't care.

The moment had come: I made it to the show. The band opened with *Song of the Century* and it was like a space ship blasting off. From 9:00 p.m. to midnight, it was the best time of my life. My older brother even told me that he wished he was there with me, but couldn't due to his commitment to the United States Navy. Aside from that, and to this very day, it was the best concert I've been to and I'll never forget it."

Alberto

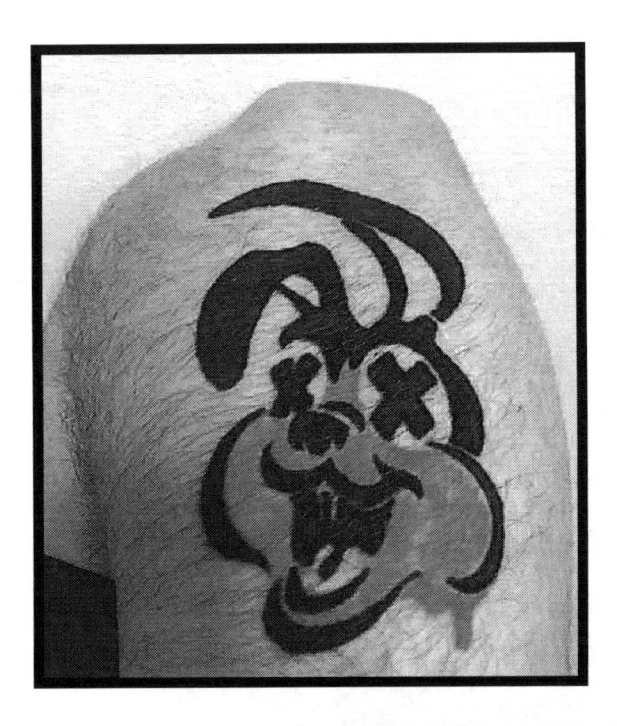

Jon Benjamin's *Awesome as Fuck* tattoo.

Jon Benjamin on stage with Green Day, 3/28/13, Rosemont, Illinois, by Mary Breeze.

Anja Everchanging and Paula Padilla with Billie Joe.

Billie Joe at Lollopalooza by Lis Booth.

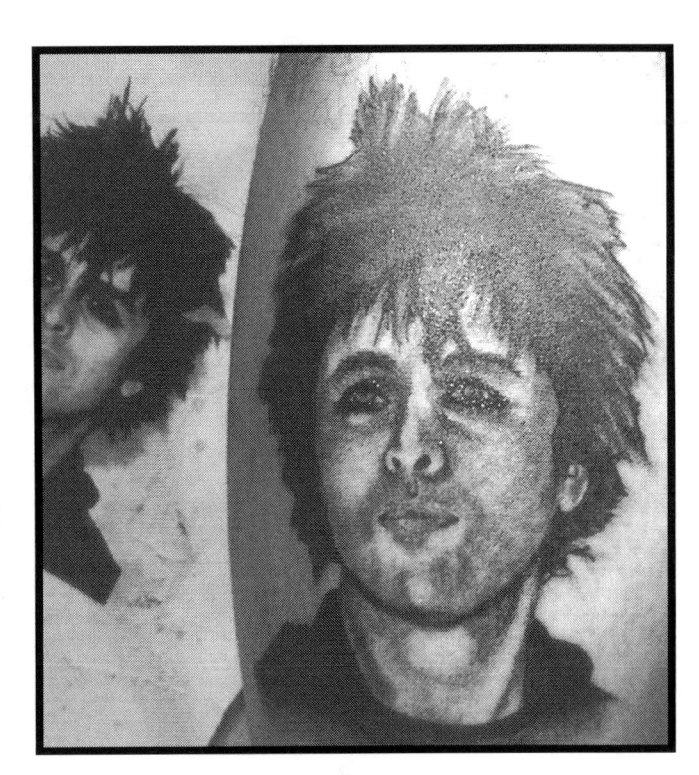

Drawing and tattoo:
Ste Fava

Luana Starke

"I was a little Brazilian girl of 11 when I first listened to Green Day. I fell in love immediately. Since then, I've become a crazy Green Day fan. This past Christmas, my mom gave me the best gift ever -- the book *Seize the Green Day!* This book inspired me to be not just another in the crowd. I haven't been to a Green Day show yet, but I hope one day to go. I'm 15 now, and when I am older I'll do like you, Niki. I read your book in one day and I really love it. My dream is meet Tré, Mike and Billie Joe and I will. Green Day changed my life. I'm very glad they have joined for the Rock and Roll Hall of Fame. They deserve it. Thank you, Luana, little dreamy Brazilian girl."

*Thank you, Luana. love~niki

Morgan Wooden

"Green Day means a whole lot to me. I saw them in 2009, on their *21st Century Breakdown* tour. I was up in front and got to touch Mike's hand. Back in 2005, I became wholly obsessed with *American Idiot*. The songs on that album helped me deal with the death of my dad. He died from esophageal cancer when I was 14. He was only 39. A friend in grief counseling also loved Green Day. We bonded over two words -- *Basket Case*.

Since 2005, I've gone on to discover all of Green Day's albums.

Green Day is much more than *just a band*.

Green Day is acceptance.

Green Day is finding your place in the world.

Thank you for being there in a time when I thought there was no way out. Thank you for making this *Whatsername* realize she matters. Thank you for being Green Day."

Victoria Schermund

"These photos are from the April 3, 2013, Green Day show in Philadelphia. My friend Tiffany, (fuzzy hat), celebrated her 21st birthday waiting in the cold with me and my other friend Gillian, (middle), to be front and center. I still tear up!!"

Gillian Malkin, Amanda Fabian, Lance, (Gillian's father), Victoria Schermund, Angie Lopez and Kay Keely. Barclay's Center, Brooklyn, New York, 4/7/13.

When Dreams Come True

by Davide Bolignano, Reggio Calabria, Italy
Story submitted by Silvia Pittoni.

"Around 2006, I took a guitar in my hands for the first time, and why? Because I started listening to Green Day! I wanted to try to play those songs that I liked so much, that I loved so much, and that fact has definitely changed my life. This soon became my biggest passion, my biggest fun. And if today I'm trying to pursue this road as a musician, this rhythmic journey that music is, it's all thanks to Green Day. This could seem like the simplest story of the world. How many guys started playing songs because they listened to their favorite band? But, believe me, for me it's real. How did I feel the night I played guitar on stage with them? I'll take you back to the Green Day concert on June 5, 2013, in Rome, Italy, at the Capannelle Hippodrome.

I was queueing in the morning of the day before the concert. I waited for many hours under the hot sun. Finally, I managed to get to the front, first central row. The emotion was so strong. I couldn't wait to see them on stage just a few steps away from me. I was having a strange feeling, like something special suddenly could have happened. In the middle of their set, after the song *Going To Pasalaqua*, Green Day started playing *Knowledge* by Operation Ivy.

I was pressed up against the barrier between the fans and the stage standing right in front of Billie Joe. I already knew that during that song the band invites a fan from the audience to play the guitar on stage. I opened my homemade poster that read, *'Let me play guitar on stage!'*

Billie Joe and Davide Bolignano.

In the middle of the song, Billie Joe started asking, 'Who knows how to play the guitar?' I immediately started jumping, calling him, trying to get his attention.

I was incredibly excited, but he went to the right side of the stage where Jason Freese pointed to a girl. Billie Joe invited her on stage. I put away my sign and said to my friend, 'It's okay, you can't have everything in life.' Except, the girl who came up on stage hugged each band member, took the microphone and said she didn't know how to play guitar. With that, Billie Joe said, 'Ciao! Arrivederci!' inviting her to get off the stage.

I re-opened my sign and started screaming and jumping to call him in every way. I was almost shaking. Billie Joe saw me, pointed at me and asked, 'Do you know how to play guitar?' I said, 'Yes, yes, yes!' The security guards pulled me out from that pit. I ran to the stage like a rocket without thinking what was happening. If I had stopped to think, I'm sure the emotion would have taken over me. It was a dream that became real. I found myself in the arms of Billie Joe. Then I played, sang, jumped and got crazy with the band. It's probably also wrong to call them *idols*. They're just people like everyone else on this planet. But, I feel like they are close to me, like friends who unknowingly have always given me great advice and made my life better. Thank you Green Day with all of my heart. I hope one day you can read these words. I love you!"

Artwork: Foxboro Freda

Foxboro Freda by Billie Joe & Billie Joe by Foxboro Freda: June, 1, 2013, Emirates Stadium in London.

Jayne Hopkins
aka
Jaynejuliannabilliejoe Armstronghomicidehopkins

"When I became a Green Day fan almost 10 years ago, I never thought they'd have such an impact on my life. They've taught me to stand up for myself and how to feel good in my own skin. I suffer with depression and if I have a bad day, listening to them always cheers me up. I never thought that, at 52, I would be going to concerts and getting such a buzz or making friends with other fans that love the band as much as I do. And, I could *never* thank them enough for all they have done for me. They are my lifesavers, heroes and inspiration. They rock my world."

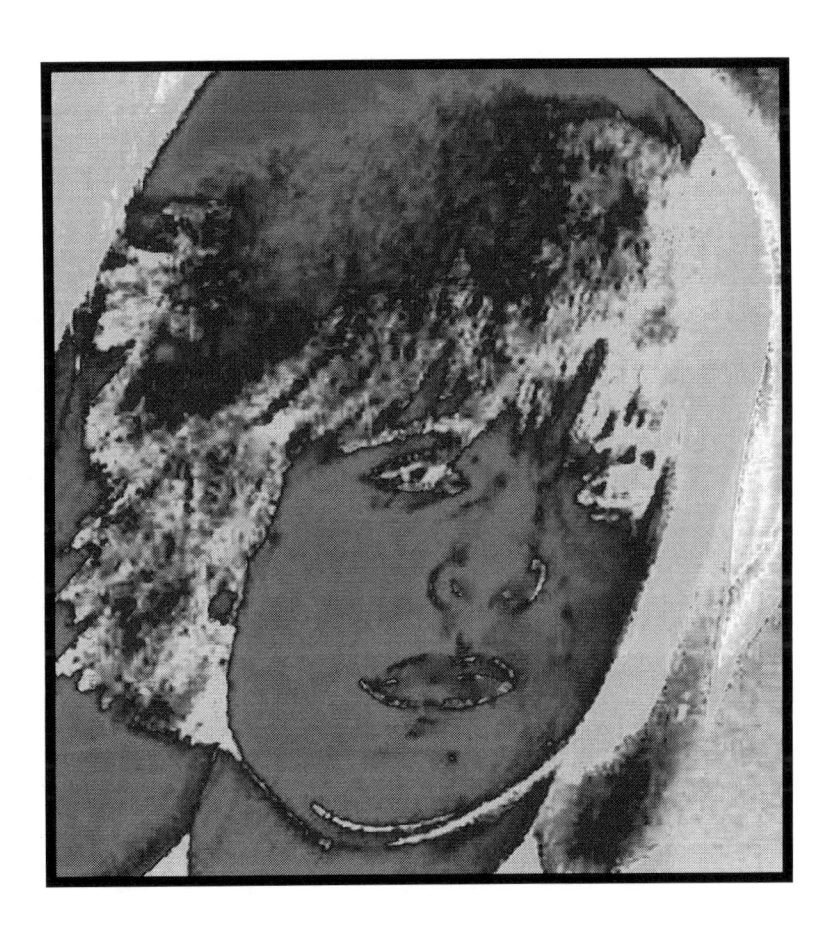

Jayne's Billie Joe tattoo.

Judy Banos receives a proposal of marriage on the set of *American Idiot*. See Billie Joe in the back?

Alessia Carlin

"Dear Green Day:

I've always been a skeptical, cold person. Not surprisingly, I've always been afraid of showing affection. So, I never imagined a band could give me such a pure, unconditional, clear and overwhelming sensation of love. Or, that I could be moved to tears by the harmony and complexity there is amongst you. The bond you share is incredible and that's what makes Green Day everlasting. Your spontaneity, positivity and determination create an intimacy that is an inspiration to everyone. Especially me. Generous artists as yourselves give fans the rare opportunity to radically change their essence. Thank you Green Day!"

Courtney Trewartha

"On September 18, 2004, I went to a small Green Day show right before *American Idiot* was released. I was about seven months pregnant with my first daughter Leah and had to get doctor approval to go. I was ok as long as I didn't go into the pit. That was fine. I was scared of the pit anyway.

I was very curious as to how my baby was going to react to the loud noises and hearing mommy scream so much. It turned out she loved it! She didn't move at all during the entire show. I figured she'd be all right because when I played *American Idiot* at home, I would hold a speaker to my belly and she would stop moving. They played *American Idiot* in its entirety and an amazing encore. As soon as the music stopped, my baby started doing flips. Two-and-a-half months later, on December 7, 2004, Leah arrived and a new generation of *Idiot* was born into my house. From the day forward, if she was cranky or just not wanting to sleep, I'd throw on *American Idiot* and lights out!

Now I have three girls who all love Green Day."

Leah

Courtney Trewartha

Courtney's Green Day Tattoos.

Nikki and Jena DiClementi

"My sister Jena DiClementi and I want to express our gratitude to Green Day for all they have done. They changed our lives in so many ways. Our mom introduced us to the band. She told Jena and me that she would take us to a Green Day show one day. But, in 2006, she was diagnosed with kidney cancer. She passed away in December 2008.

Exactly seven months later, on July 13, 2009, we went to our first Green Day show in Chicago at the United Center. Since then, we've seen them multiple times in Illinois and around the country. This band means everything to us. Whatever mood or situation we are in, Green Day always makes things better. They have inspired us to express ourselves making the two of us stronger. We are proud Green Day fans and nothing can ever top them. Hopefully, we will meet these phenomenal men someday."

Best friend Lizard, left, with Jena and Nikki July 13, 2009, United Center, Chicago.

-The rooms of Nikki and Jena DiClementi-

168

--A Thank you--

"Holding a copy of *21st Century Breakdown* in my hands was like holding a day pass to heaven: I knew pure bliss awaited me, yet I was paralyzed by the thought of cashing it in. I mean, how does one prepare for a trip to paradise? I wanted to make sure that I was in the right frame of mind to receive the blessing from the Rock and Roll Gods. After all, heaven would be squandered on a person in a bad mood or someone who is cranky.

Despite my reservations, I finally put on the CD. With the lights turned off, I pressed play and prepared for transcendence. From the first note, I knew it was going to be everything I'd hoped for. Elated, I listened to the whole album in one sitting. Every track created its' own feeling of euphoria. As the chorus for *Viva La Gloria* started, tears streamed down my face and I sensed that my father, who had passed away, was in the room with me experiencing this pop perfection.

Thank you Green Day for your commitment to awesomeness. I appreciate you tremendously.

Love, Riley the Disappearing Boy."

Eleonora Longo

"It's been over 10 years since I'm a fan now. I'm Italian so I bet you know how many misadventures we had with Green Day's shows. We got our reward in 2013 during the *99 Revolutions* Tour. I saved money for months, waited and gave all my best to help these dreams come true.

I saw them many times in 2013 through Italy and Switzerland. I took planes, trains and pullman [bus]. I've slept outside of the gates in rain, hailstones and wind. I've been reunited with old friends that are part of the Green Day family and have met new ones. I've hugged Billie Joe, smiled at Mike and talked to Tré. I've thanked all the people who work with them. I made a Green Day flag and brought it to their shows. Seeing Billie smiling and looking into my eyes was one of the most exciting experiences ever.

Eleonora Longo third from left above Mike Dirnt's head.

I want to thank these guys for what they have created. If it wasn't for them I wouldn't be writing this! I can't wait to see and hug them again.

P.S. - I'm so proud of them."

Photo: Eleonora Longo

Sarah, Fanny, Joanie from Quebec, Canada, and Yvana from Belgium at the Main Square Festival in Arras, France, 2013.

Joanie Pothier

"We had the chance to go to a couple of shows from the *99 Revolutions* tour in North America and Europe. We had a blast! It's so amazing to see Green Day in concert because they are passionate and genuinely happy sharing those moments with their fans. Congratulations for their induction to the Rock & Roll Hall of Fame, from the bottom of our hearts, thank you!"

Desensitized Brat
Owner *Green Day Collections*--Instagram

"My name is Janine. I've been a Green Day fan since 1994. My friends' parents ordered us Pay-Per-View to watch *Woodstock 2* and I was hooked. My first show was in 1995 and I swore my first tattoo would be a Green Day tattoo. I *really* wanted to get a tattoo as soon as I turned 18 but couldn't decide on an image. So I put it off.

Years went by and I kept getting more tattoos. I still couldn't commit to just one Green Day image that summed up my now decade-plus-love. Last year, 2014, marked 20 years of me being a fan and I finally decided that if I couldn't choose one image, I'd get them all! I got a half-sleeve showcasing various Green Day images through the years. I hope to one day make it a full-sleeve.

On October 3, 2010, my sister took me to see *American Idiot* on Broadway. It was the second time I'd seen the show and the first time with Billie Joe playing the role of *St. Jimmy*. Before leaving the house that day, I grabbed a red Sharpie and swore I'd be returning with his signature.

After the show, it was raining and the doors to the theater were crowded with fans. I'm too short to see over people, so we called it a night. My sister brought the car around to meet me on the sidewalk: she is not a Green Day fan at all. The two of us were in the car out in the rain and I remembered how I'd told people I was going to meet Billie Joe.

My sister grabbed a camera and we started taking selfies with various surprised, shocked and awestruck faces. We decided we'd tell people we met him but we couldn't get a good picture. We made complete fools of ourselves in the car that night, and, when we were done, *Billie Joe's car drove passed us!*

I don't know what got into my sister, but she followed the car. It drove around the block. Billie Joe and Adrienne got out. I didn't know what I should/could do. I watched them walk away until my sister literally pushed me out of the car saying, 'GO!!!!'

Janine with Sharpee and Billie Joe.

I barely got my foot on the sidewalk before a security guard pushed me back into the street. Aggressively, my sister yelled from the car, *'Don't let that man touch you. He is not to put his hands on you unless you attempt to touch Billie Joe.'* I asked the security guard if that was true and he dropped his arm letting me run up to Billie Joe. He agreed to take a photo and sign my autograph book but he was concerned a crowd would form. When we were done, he said he wanted to duck out fast. I got nervous and snapped my picture too soon. He knew it and suggested I take another one really quickly. But a crowd started to form and was growing. I felt bad and declined to waste any more of his time.

He totally got his spit on my Sharpie!

My sister and I had spent an hour that afternoon taking awful selfies so we could tell our family we met Billie Joe. We were going to tell people the reason the pictures were so bad was that so many people were around him. In the end, that's exactly what happened. It was the greatest night ever, not just because of Billie Joe, but because I've never hung out with my sister like that. She went above and beyond to make sure I enjoyed every moment. Now, she's either secretly become a Green Day fan, or she's aching for a repeat, cuz she's booked a trip for us to attend the band's induction ceremony at the Rock and Roll Hall of Fame! More adventures await us."

Rock and Roll Hall of Fame Induction Week
-Cleveland, Ohio, USA.-

Avalon Folmsbee

Cleveland House of Blues,
April 16, 2015.
Photo: Kerry Vail

Rock and Roll Boulevard, Downtown Cleveland.
Photo: Cheryl McCloskey, New York

"The things that this band can do. I've met fans from around the world this past week and they all have a story. The *Idiot Nation* boasts members of every age, shape, color and size. We are a true family. We look out for each other. When Green Day comes to town, we reunite and it's wonderful. To watch the band being inducted into the Rock and Roll Hall of Fame is something I'll never forget. I better thank my lucky stars I was in Cleveland to witness this amazing honor. Thank you Green Day. Thank you *Idiots*."

Ian Ries, Kentucky

Kerry Vail came from North Carolina.

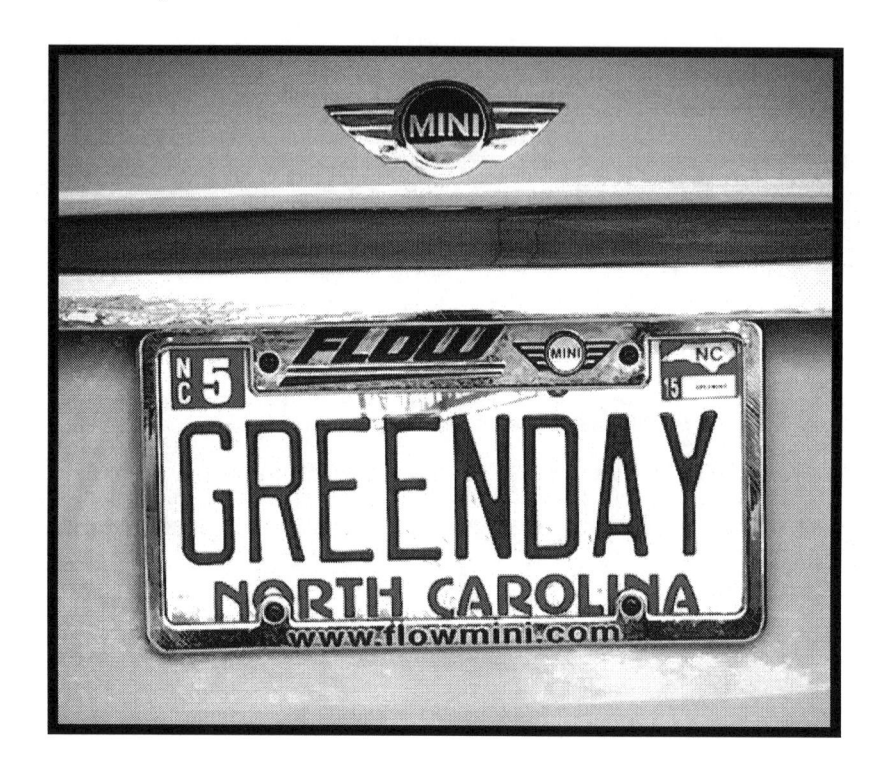

Fans from Pennsylvania got famous when TV crews and reporters noticed their campsite. They waited outside The House of Blues for the Green Day show 24 hours later and succeeded in claiming their rightful place in the front row.

Beth Wieman, St. Louis, and Cheryl McCloskey, New York, waiting in line outside the House of Blues.
Photo: Shannon Connors

Graham Mitchell, England, Shannon Connors, Pennsylvania, and Chris Wieman, St. Louis.
Photo: Beffy Wieman

Eileen Pretzel, New York, Diane Merz, in her Adeline hoodie, Washington, and Katie McPansy Grogan, Kansas.

Number 20 in line!
Nikki & her sister Jena DiClementi, Illinois.

Nikki DiClementi

"After a six hour road trip, my dad went to our hotel room to sleep while my sister Jena and I camped out for the Green Day show at the House of Blues. It was 4:30 a.m. I had a ticket but it wasn't guaranteed that Jena could get into the show. This would be the first time I'd see Green Day without her.

We tried getting her a ticket during the pre-sale and the public sale. We asked other fans online. We even signed up for the *Idiot Nation* contest. But there was no luck.

We were hoping for a miracle that day.

Then Green Day magic happened.

The House of Blues was able to score a ticket for my sister and she was able to go in with me! It felt like I'd won the lottery.

It has been a dream to see my ultimate favorite band in a small venue. Rumor had it that Sweet Children [Green Day's original name with band members Billie Joe, Mike and John Kiffmeyer] was going to be play the show. And the rumors were true. They played so many of my favorites.

Green Day deserves to be in the Hall of Fame and I am honored to have been there to celebrate with them. One of my bucket-list wishes was to see a Beatle and Joan Jett perform sometime in my life. On April 18th, I got to see both and Green Day. I can't wait to see what the future holds for our boys."

Twilight in Cleveland.
Photo: Cheryl McCloskey

–House of Blues, 4-16-15–
Act 1: Sweet Children

Blue
Photo: Kerry Vail

Sweet Children drummer, John Kiffmeyer.
Photo: Eileen Pretzel

Sweet Children.
Photo: Katie McPansy Grogan

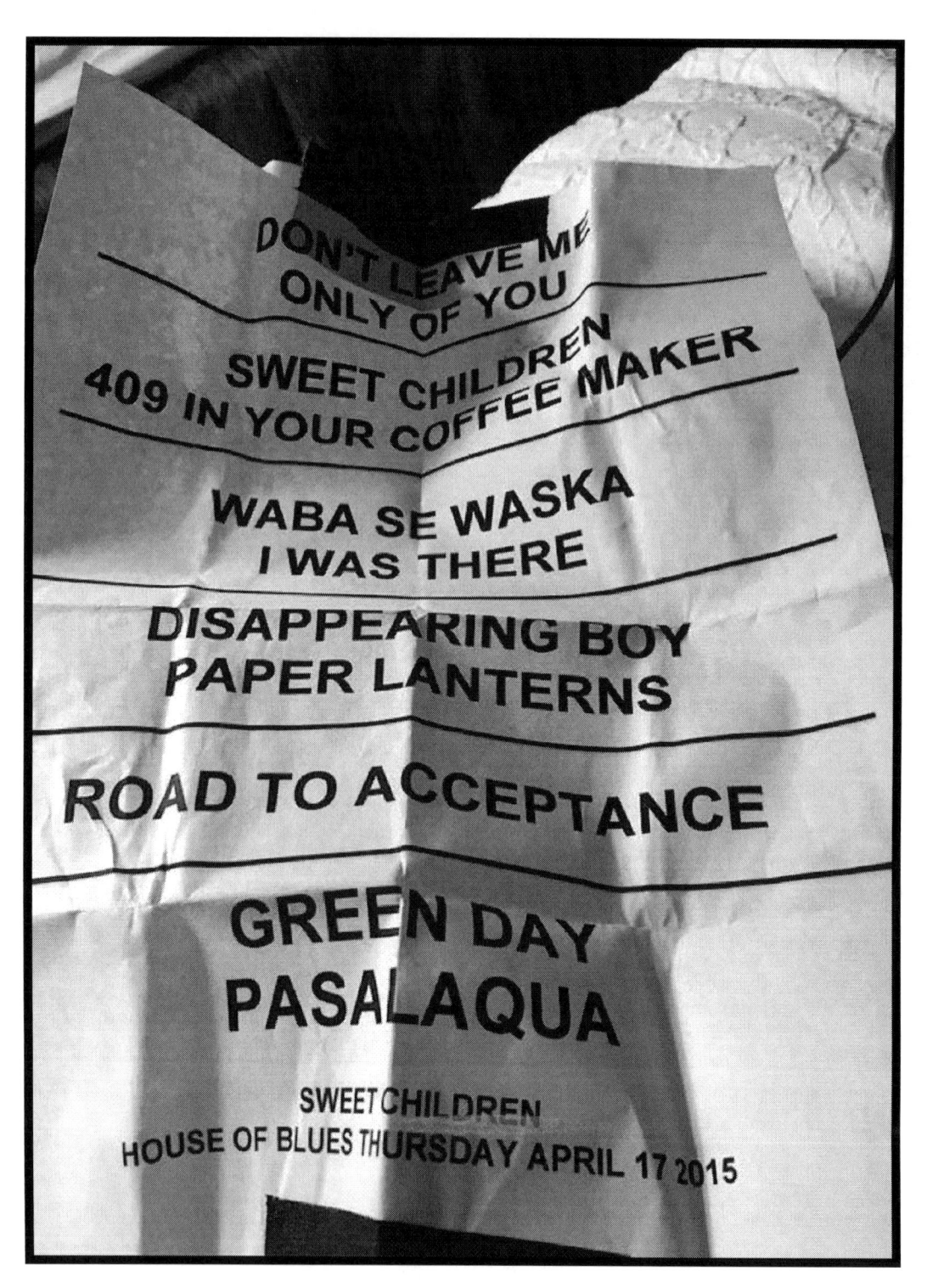

Sweet Children set list.
Photo: Ian Ries

Sweet Children, House of Blues.
Photo: Taylor Bellville, Ohio

–Live at the House of Blues, 4-16-15–
Act 2: Green Day

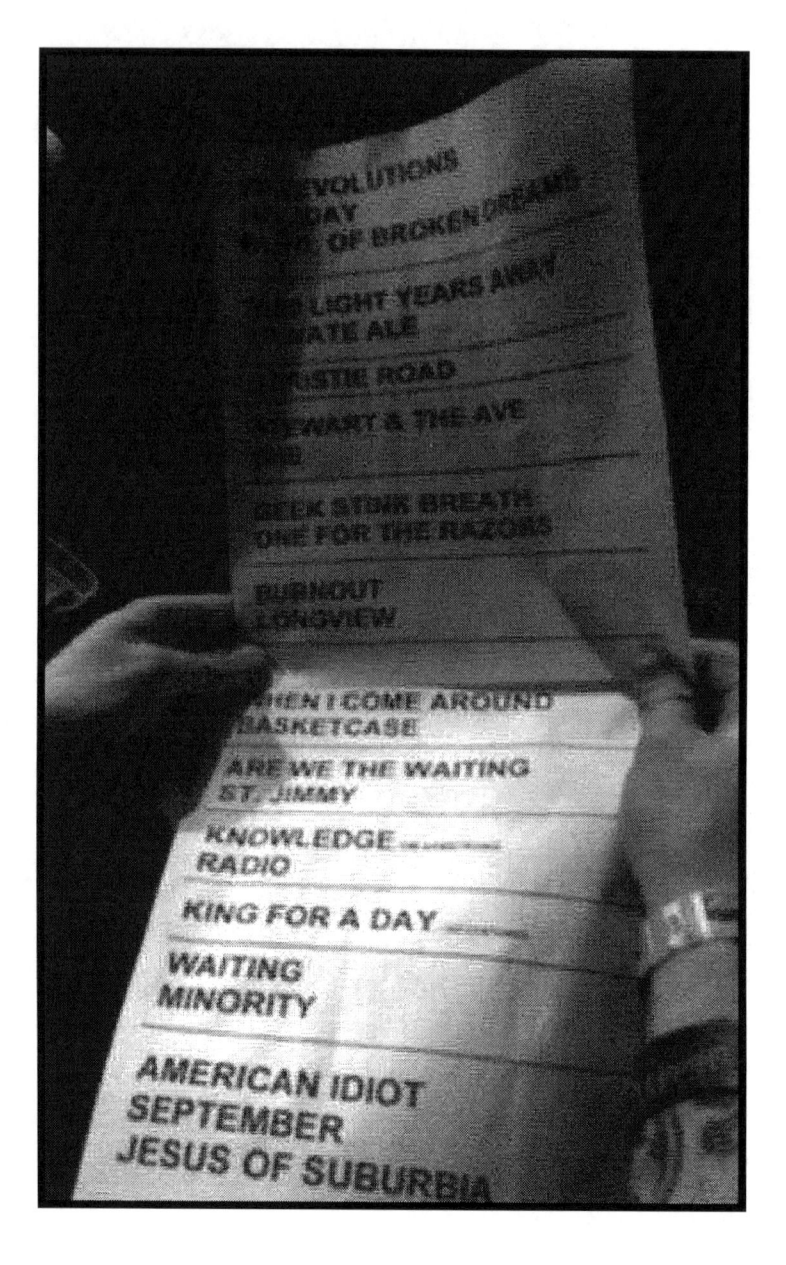

Green Day set list.
Photo: Eileen Pretzel

Billie Joe
Photo: Angie Griffin, Louisiana

Jason White
Photo: Ian Ries

Jason White
Photo: Eileen Pretzel

Billie Joe and Mike.
Photo: Taylor Bellville

My Trip to Cleveland
by Niki Lee

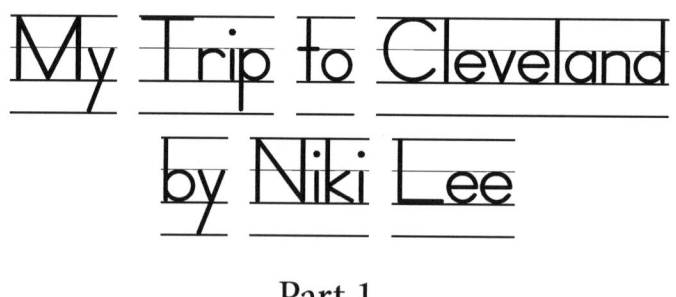

Part 1

Arriving in Cleveland the morning of April 17th, I met Eileen Pretzel at her hotel. She'd invited me to share a room with her for the weekend. After exchanging pleasantries, she expressed concern over something Billie Joe said the night before at The House of Blues:

Huh?

I watched a video from show. It was weird. At that exact moment, I got an email from Italian Green Day fan Davide Boligno.

"Hey Niki! I'm freaking out a little bit because of what Billie Joe said at the concert last night.

'This is right now, this is a very special night for us, because this is the closest I'm gonna get to you for a long while.'

What do you think about it? I only hope he didn't hint at a retirement. Will you keep us informed from inside the Rock Hall? Thank you!"

I had no idea what it meant.

Refreshed after my red-eye flight, Eileen and I joined a bunch of fans at the Hall of Fame Museum and tried to see as much as we could. Besides the exhibits, everyone was buzzing about Billie Joe's comment from the night before. No one knew what it meant. But they were sad.

Um...wha-what?

Me heading to the Rock and Roll Hall of Fame, 4-17-15.

Photo: Eileen Pretzel

Evolution of Rock.
Photo: me

Diane Merz, Karen Katz Reta, Dorie Watts,
Cheryl McCloskey, Shannon Connors, me, Beth Wieman, Eileen Pretzel
and Briana Treasger in front of the inductees' exhibits.

(The Green Day exhibit was tough to photograph due to glare from lighting. I included different angles. The plaque on the next page explains GD's exhibit.)

Photo: me

Mike Dirnt Bass Guitar
Kramer Custom, c. 1974
Collection of Green Day

Childhood friends Billie Joe Armstrong and Mike Dirnt formed their first band when they were 14 years old. "As a band, ever since Billie and I were just little kids, we've always had a really good work ethic," Dirnt recalled. "I always felt like, whatever you're going to do, do it to the best of your ability, and if you're lucky, it will be what you do best!" Dirnt played this bass at the band's triumphant appearance at the Woodstock '94 Festival on August 14, 1994.

Tré Cool Drum Kit, c. 2001
Collection of Green Day

Tré Cool replaced Green Day's original drummer, John Kiffmeyer in 1990. Cool recalled about joining the band, "I had trouble fitting in, in a musical sense...When I started, I had too many drums.... It took me a while to get it... I started figuring out how to make the band a stronger unit, to make it jump." This kit was set afire in an act of exuberant performance art at the conclusion of Green Day's set during a performance at RFK Stadium in Washington, DC, May 27, 2001.

Billie Joe Armstrong Guitar
1956 Gibson Les Paul Junior
Collection of Green Day

"It has always been about doing things your own way, what it represents to me is ultimate freedom and a sense of individuality," Billie Joe Armstrong said. "Music is the air that I breathe, it's the blood that pumps through my veins." Armstrong used this guitar on the *American Idiot* recording sessions and tours.

Billie Joe Armstrong Outfit, 1994
Collection of Green Day

Billie Joe Armstrong wore this outfit during Green Day's performance at Woodstock '94 in Saugerties, New York. Woodstock '94 was nicknamed Mudstock, partly due to Green Day's performance. Days of rain turned the venue into a field of mud, and as Armstrong taunted the audience with "I don't care what you do, I don't want to be a mud hippie like you," an enormous mudfight ensued. Fans rushed the stage and bassist Mike Dirnt lost three teeth in the melee. "It was the closest thing to total chaos I've ever seen in my life," Armstrong recalled. "Technically, it was a human disaster."

Meghan E Tierney in her *Insomniac* T-Shirt.

Photo: Eileen Pretzel

Photo: Traci Roll Schaum, Indiana

Photo: Traci Roll Schaum

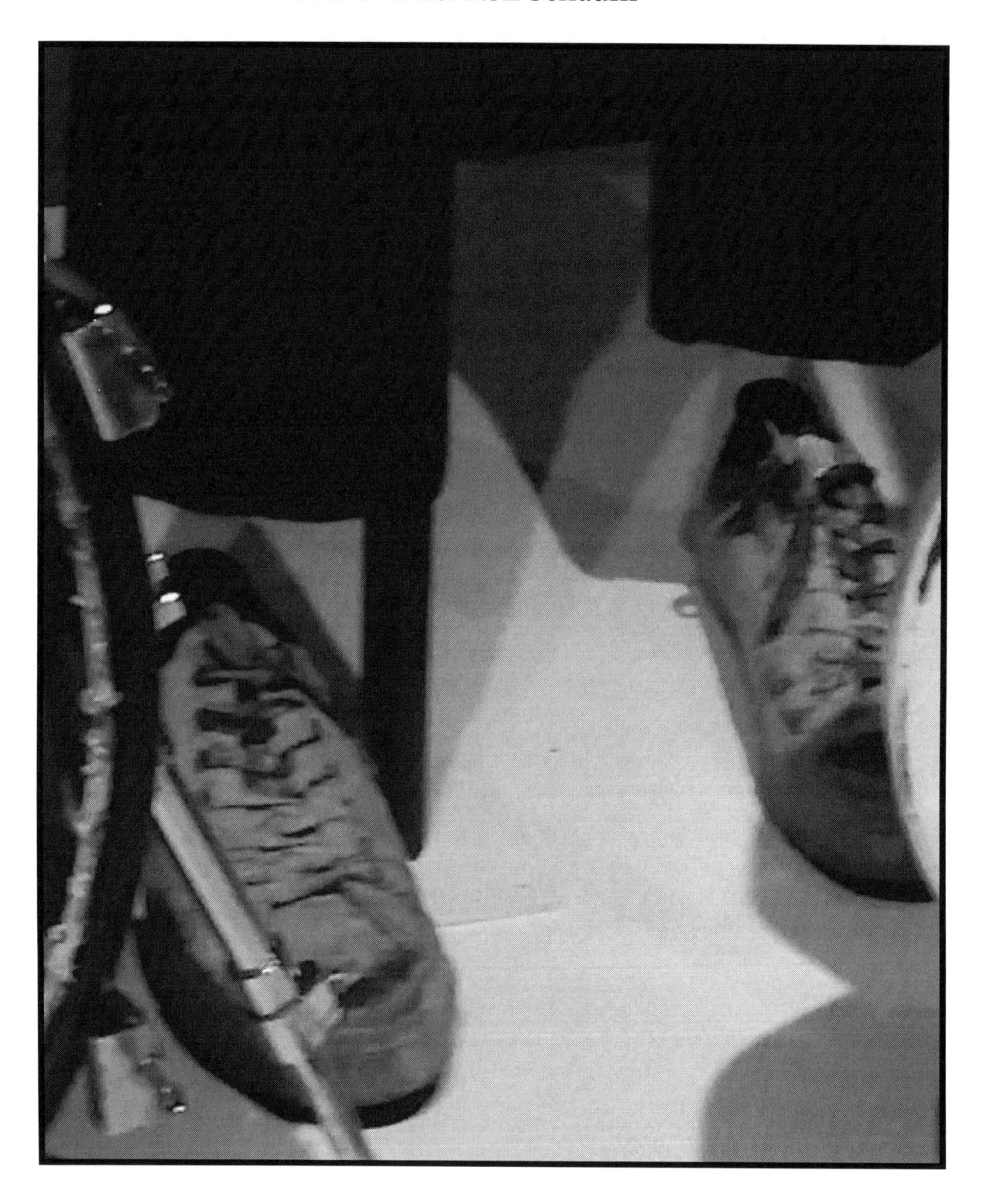

Billie Joe's homework--1981
Photo: me

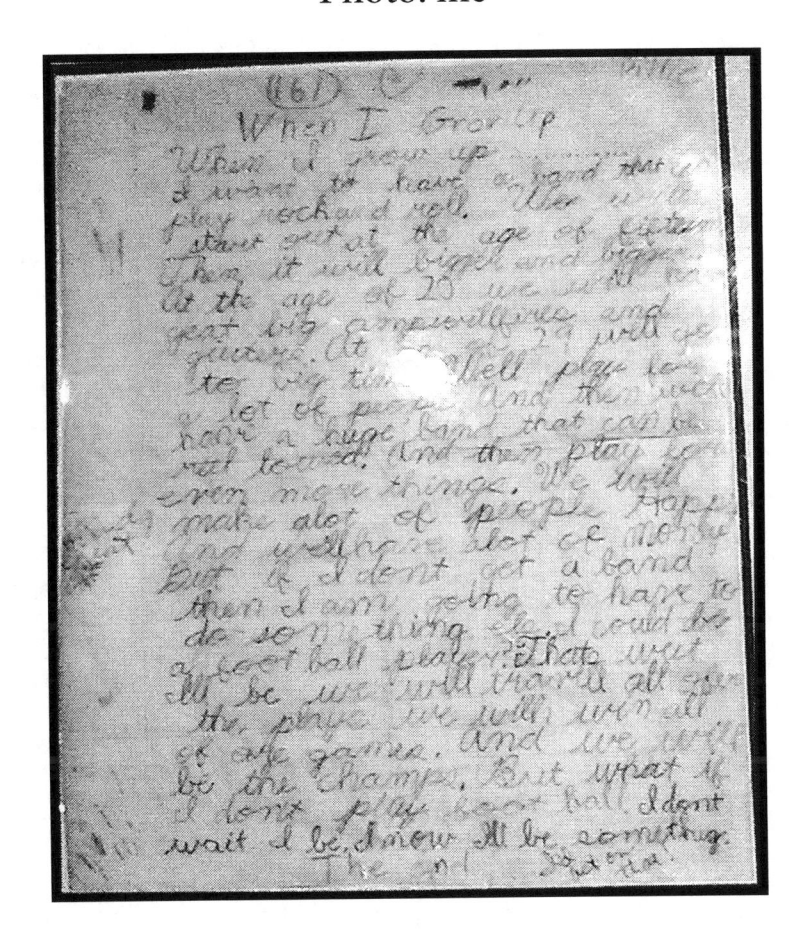

When I Grow Up
by Billie Joe Armstrong

"When I grow up I want to have a band that can play rock and roll. We will start out at the age of fifteen. Then it will [get] bigger and bigger. At the age of 20 we will have great big amplwillfires and guiters. At the age of 29 we'll go to big time.

We'll play for a lot of people. And then we'll have a huge band that can be reel loved. And then play for even more things. We'll make alot of people happy and we will have alot of money.

But if I don't get a band then I am going to have to do something else. I could be a football player. That's what I'll be. We will travel all ofer the plays. We will win all of the games. And we will be the champs. But what if I don't play football. I don't know what I'll be. I know I'll be something."

Teachers Note: "I'd bet on that!"

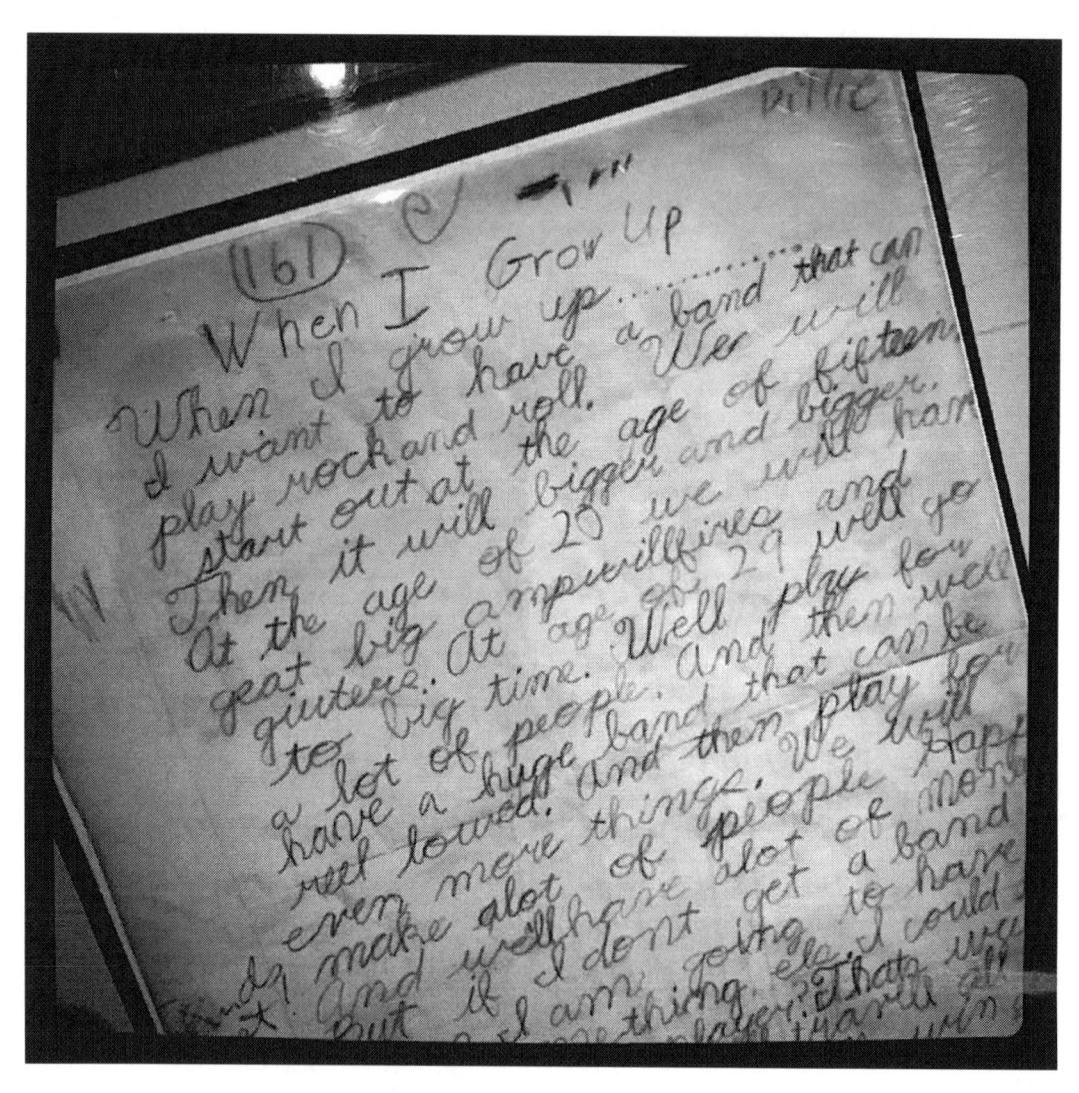

Photo: Meghan E Turner, New York

My Trip to Cleveland

Part 2

The bottom floor of the Rock and Roll Hall of Fame houses glass cases filled with Beatles memorabilia. Gazing at a John Lennon guitar, I noticed Beck checking it out as well. I tried getting a photo of the back of his head. Hey, back of the head is better than none. While pretending to look at the exhibit, I pointed my camera at him. As I went to shoot, a plain-clothed security guard barked,

"No pictures!"

And I thought I'd been so slick.

"How did you know that I was about to take a picture of him?" I asked.

"Your eyes lit up," he replied.

Busted.

Photo: Meghan E Tierney

Fallyn Ruzzi, New York, and Ringo's drum kit.

An acoustic guitar belonging to
John Lennon.
Photo: Meghan E Tierney

Dave Grohl and Meghan E Tierney.
No big deal...

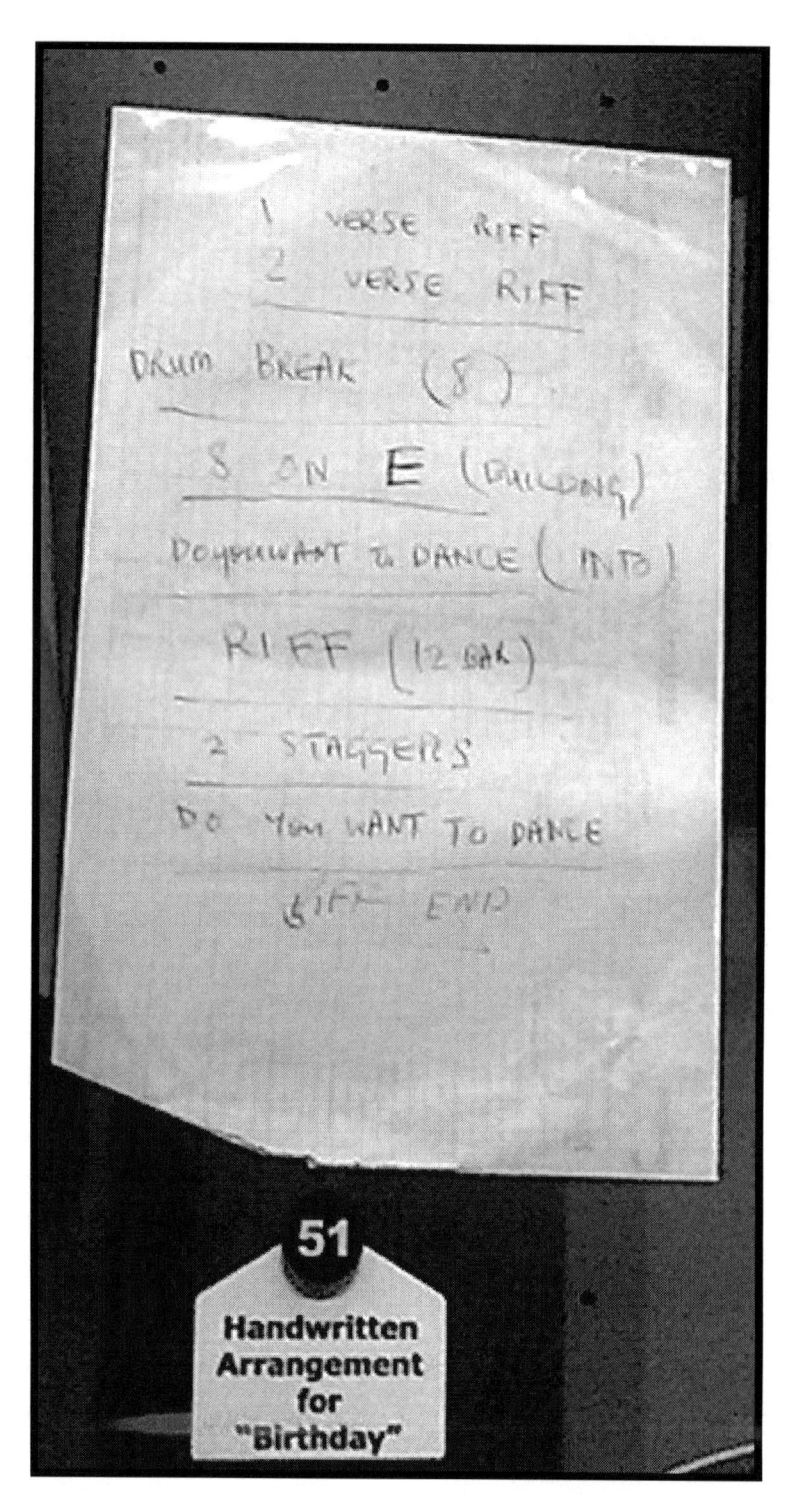

Handwritten chart of the
Beatles' *Birthday*.
Photo: me

American Idiot director Michael Mayer and Denise. Denise picked the right day to wear her *A.I.* hoodie.

Michael Mayer, Eileen Pretzel and Larry Livermore.

Larry Livermore sent this laminate to Louis Lasande in Paris.

Angie Insomniac Lopez and Nancy Allen at the Hard Rock in Cleveland.

After our museum tour, we had a brief break before a meet-up with our comrades at the Hard Rock, downtown Cleveland. The affair had been well planned by Nancy Allen from Minnesota.

Angie Griffin and me at the Hard Rock.

Angie Insomnic Lopez

Photos:
Taylar Kent,
Nebraska

The Hard Rock had booked a Green Day tribute band for us: Average Joe. When they played *Good Riddance* we put our arms around each other and sang.

My Trip to Cleveland

Part 3

Chris Grebinski-Policicchio and her ticket.

Billie Joe hugging Bridget Lantz on the Red Carpet.
Photo: Traci Roll Schaum

After their appearance on the Red Carpet, Green Day headed to their fans.

Tré Cool by Taylar Kent.

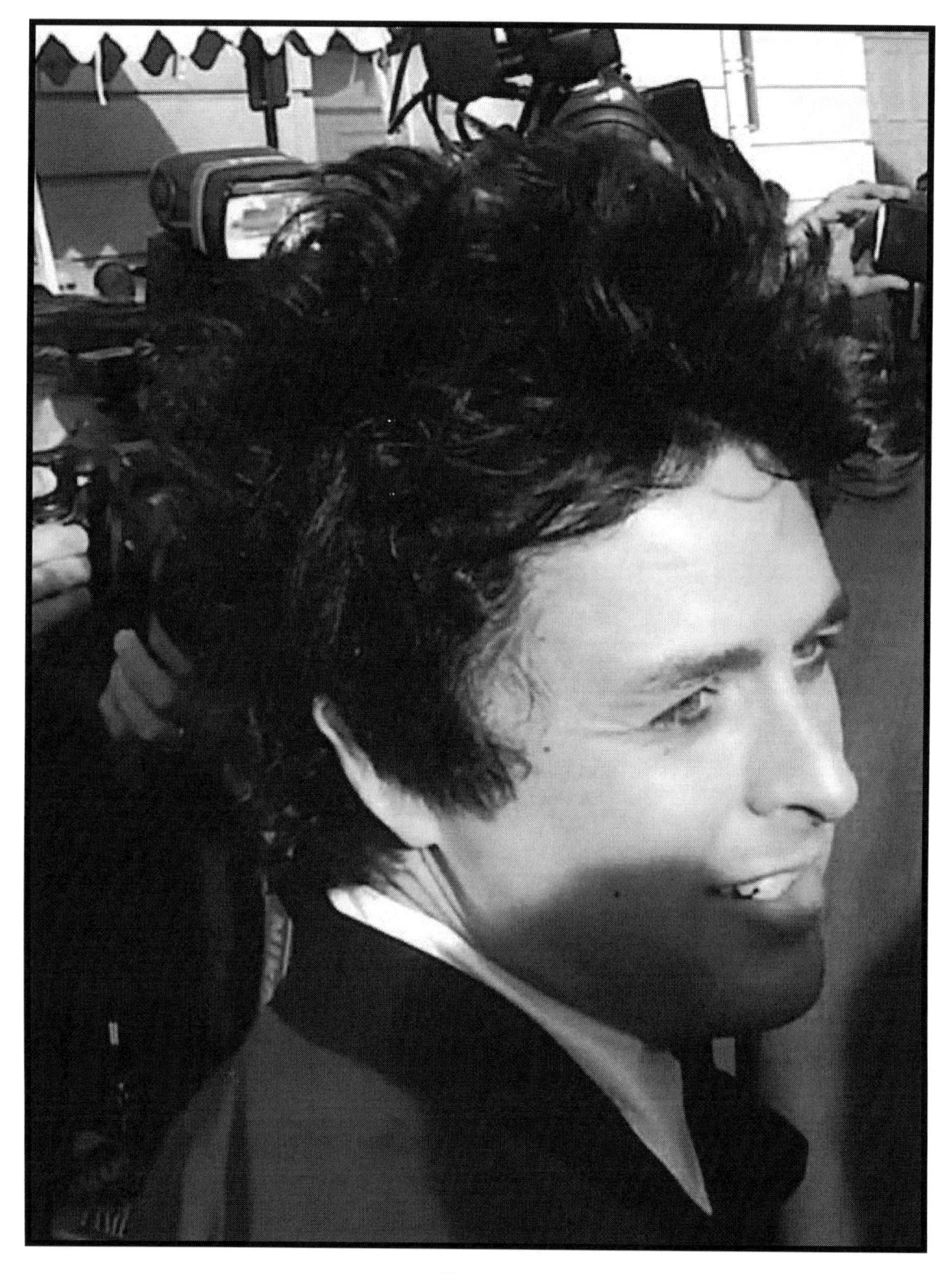

Billie Joe
Photo: Angie Griffin

Outside and inside Cleveland Public Hall by Chris Grebinski-Policicchio.

A simulcast of the ceremony was held inside the Rock and Roll Hall of Fame Museum. Public Hall was two blocks away.

Photos:
Taylar Kent

Once inside, the show began promptly at 7:30 p.m.

When I saw Green Day photos splash across the jumbo stage screen, I jumped out of my seat and ran to the empty aisle between the lower balcony and the upper balcony. Seconds later, Eileen joined me. We had a perfect view and room to dance. Security made a half-hearted attempt to boot us back to our seats and then left us alone.

Photo: Angie Griffin

Green Day making their acceptance speeches.
Photo: Nancy Allen

The band took to the stage and each gave grateful acceptance speeches. At the end of Mike's, he cleared up the mystery of Billie Joe's *'I'm not going to be seeing you for a while'* comment at the House of Blues when he said,

'See ya at band practice!'

There was an audible sigh of relief and then applause. They weren't going anywhere.

Paul McCartney *"inducing"* Ringo Starr.
Photo: Katie McPansy Grogan

Photo:
Eileen Pretzel

RINGO!!

Photo:
Meghan E Tierney

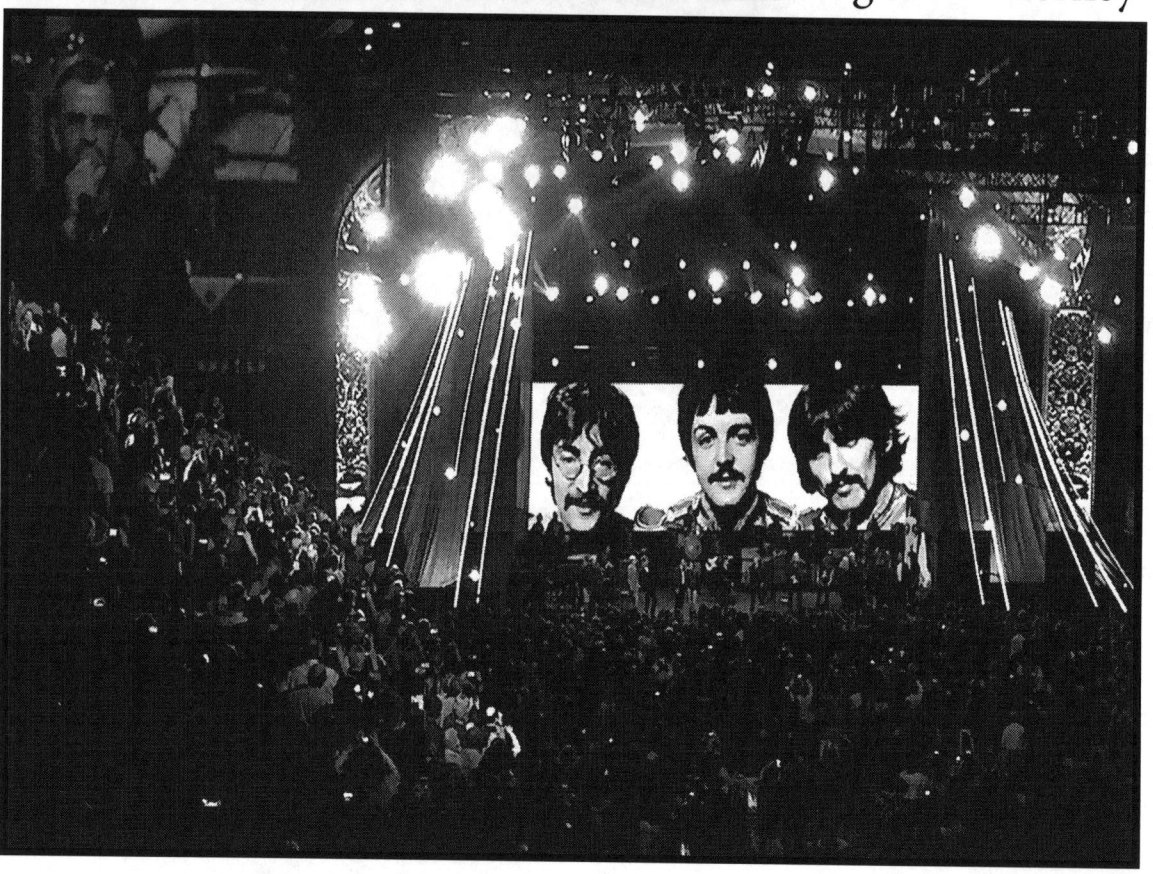

Finally, Paul McCartney took the stage and joked that he was happy to "induce" Ringo Starr for his stellar solo career spanning 40 years. After Ringo's speech, he invited Green Day on stage to play the song *Boys*. I didn't know what to do I was so happy! Tears were rolling as I smiled a giant smile.

For the finale, Ringo and Paul were joined by all of the inductees. They launched into *With a Little Help From My Friends* and *I Wanna be Your Man*.

When they were done, Ringo and Paul clasped hands and bowed, Beatles' style. "That's the end of it," Ringo said heading off into the dark.

Photo: Eileen Pretzel

The next morning, I messaged Davide from Italy to tell him Green Day wasn't retiring. He wrote back:

"You make me so thrill! Beautiful words that you told me! It fills me with joy."

Later that morning, Billie Joe posted this:

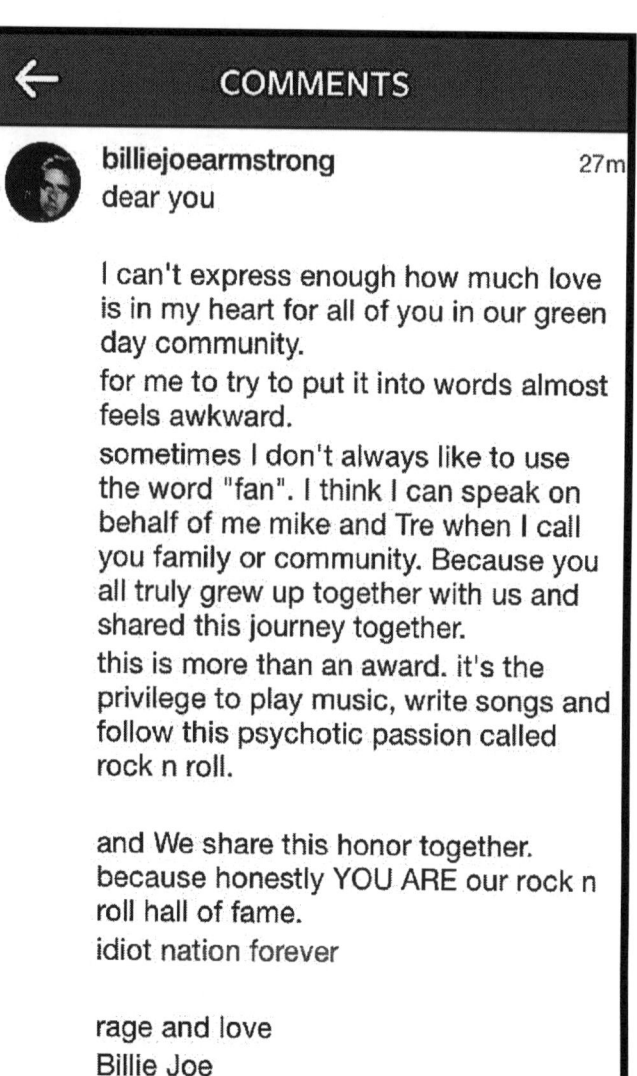

> **billiejoearmstrong** 27m
> dear you
>
> I can't express enough how much love is in my heart for all of you in our green day community.
> for me to try to put it into words almost feels awkward.
> sometimes I don't always like to use the word "fan". I think I can speak on behalf of me mike and Tre when I call you family or community. Because you all truly grew up together with us and shared this journey together.
> this is more than an award. it's the privilege to play music, write songs and follow this psychotic passion called rock n roll.
>
> and We share this honor together. because honestly YOU ARE our rock n roll hall of fame.
> idiot nation forever
>
> rage and love
> Billie Joe

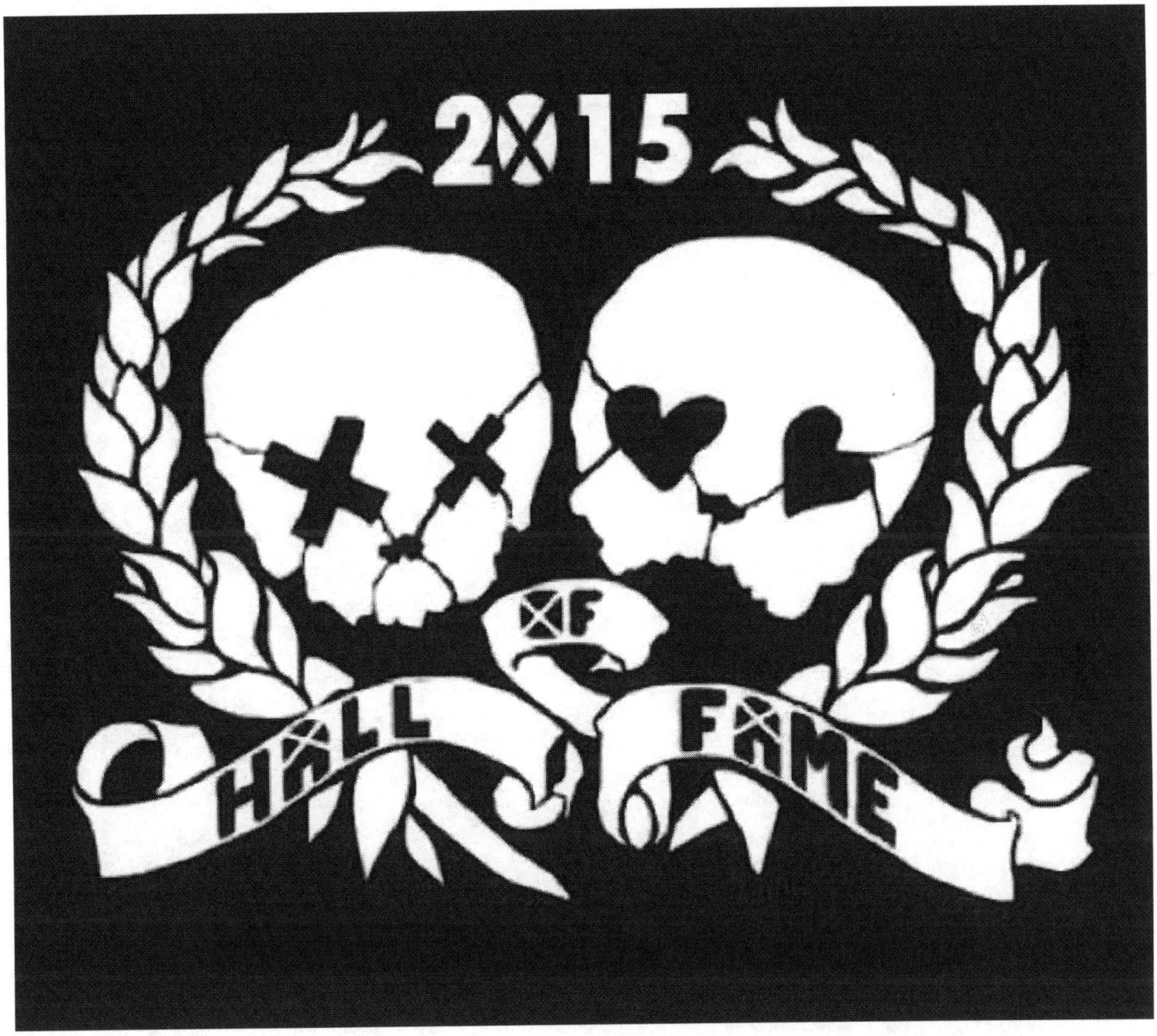
2015
HALL
OF
FAME

MORE STUFF...

Photo: Sandy Hicks Barber, Missouri.

Sharon Mitchell

"Green Day are so much more than just a band. Yes, their music touches our hearts and their lyrics open our minds, but there's more. My husband Graham and I were in Cleveland to celebrate their achievement. I met fans from their 20s to their 60s. We will travel to places we've never been to see our guys. We will forego a holiday or new pair of winter boots to buy ticket to a show.

One fan traveled from Australia to the ceremony but she didn't have a ticket. By the time she reached Cleveland, we'd gotten her one. That's the Green Day magic. We're a community of like-minded souls and unite not only to see the band, but to catch up. In the past year, Graham and I attended two weddings and several *Idiot* parties. My home, *Longview,* is always open as base-camp for Green Day fans when the band tours the UK. The record of people crashing here is 27 in 2009.

Billie Joe, Mike and Tré always refer to each other as brothers and I am proud and delighted to be a member of their *Idiot Family*."

Sharon next to her puppy amidst *family* at *Longview.*

Sarah Lemke

"I finally got Billie Joe to sign the portrait I drew of him. *Sorry I got Sharpie on your thumb and thank you for not getting pissed at me Billie Joe!*

The night of the Hall of Fame ceremony, Green Day made a grand gesture by stepping off the Red Carpet to talk to fans. They were the only artists who did. Next time someone asks why you love the band, this is a very good reason.

Congratulations you guys and thank you for these last few amazing days. You deserve all the honors you have gotten and will continue to get. I love you Green Day!"

Courtney Trewartha, Michigan, and Sarah Lemke, Wisconsin, with Sarah's signed portrait of Billie Joe, 4-18-15.

Bridget Lantz

"I've been a die-hard Green Day fan for eight years. They've helped me so much. I've never felt that I 'belonged.' Green Day showed me I had a place.

On April 18, 2015, I was at the Red Carpet entrance to the Rock and Roll Hall of Fame ceremony waiting for Green Day. Three cars pulled up and then I heard a massive scream. Out stepped Billie Joe, Mike and Tré to mass hysteria. After the Red Carpet, they came over to us fans taking pictures and signing autographs. I hugged my hero Billie Joe! Life has never been better."

Bridget Lantz, Illinois, and Mike Dirnt at the Red Carpet.
Photo: Traci Roll Schaum

Miley Cyrus Inducting Joan Jett.
Photo: Eileen Pretzel

Naomi Lir, Toronto, Ontario.
Signed portrait.

Cammy Heggie, Glasgow, Scotland.
Tattooed arm.

Anne Solek, New Jersey, and
J'net Newton, Tulsa, Oklahoma.

Cullen Logan and Billie Joe.

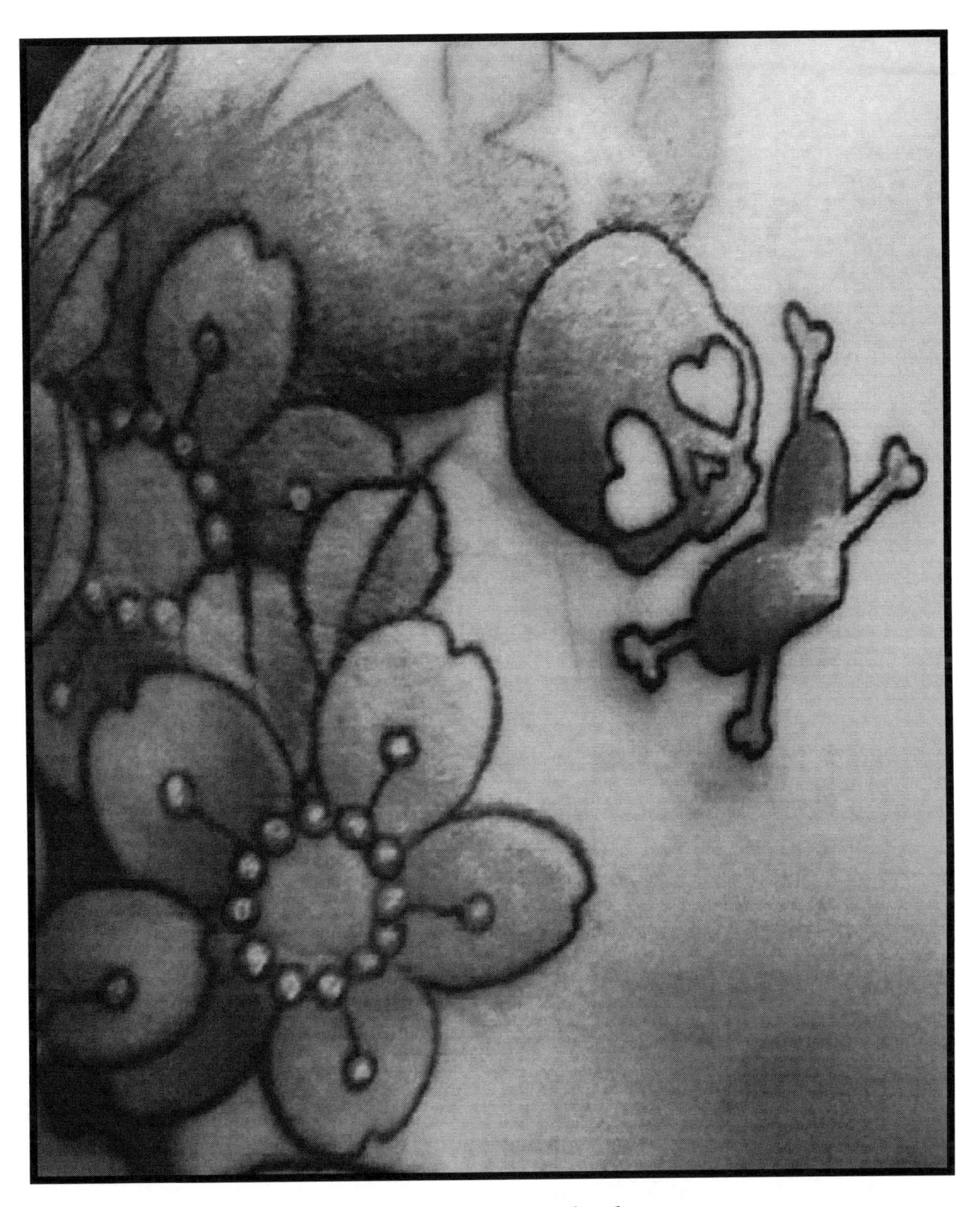

Karen Barker, England.
Tattoo Artist: Adeline Tattoo

Chris Grebinski-Policicchio

"When it was announced that Green Day would be inducted into the Rock and Roll Hall of Fame, a huge group of international fans began making plans for Cleveland. We coordinated meet-ups and hang outs and I planned on buying tickets to the live simulcast of the ceremony when I arrived.

On April 18th, I hit the road to Cleveland with my husband John. On the drive, I got in touch with New York Green Day fan/friend Tanya Elder. She said she'd find me a ticket to the simulcast. My husband isn't as big a fan as I am, so he made other plans which was fine for both of us. Within minutes, Tanya found me a ticket through mutual GD friends Beth Wieman and Shannon Connors. But, not for the simulcast... for the actual ceremony! I blame it on the Green Day magic everyone talks about.

We landed in the hotel parking lot and I immediately saw the purple-haired head of Sharon Lynne Mitchell. I've been Facebook friends with Sharon for five years and we'd never met. I ran up to her and her husband Graham and we hugged and cried. Meeting and reuniting with friends is as special as the main event. We all planned to meet at the Red Carpet outside Cleveland Public Hall before the ceremony. Then John and I went to check out the museum.

Chris Grebinski-Policicchio, Michigan, and Meghan Bacchus, New York.

Chris and Deirdre Adams, Michigan.

Me and Chris.

Inside the museum, we headed straight to the Green Day exhibit. There was a homework essay by Billie Joe alongside handwritten lyrics to Green Day songs. They had BJ's mud-covered outfit from Woodstock '94 next to Tre's burnt drums. It was unreal. We ran into Tanya and grabbed a beer and had another *Idiot* reunion. Milling around the joint was Eileen Pretzel, Bethany Moriah, Deirdre Adams, Megan Bacchus, Katie Grogan, Sharon, Cheryl McCloskey and Courtney Trewartha and Jill Terrill. The best.

Cleveland Public Hall was huge and I was way in the back at the very top. The inductees were: Green Day, Bill Withers, Stevie Ray Vaughan and Double Trouble, Lou Reed, Joan Jett and the Blackhearts, The 5 Royales, The Paul Butterfield Blues Band and Ringo Starr. *Ringo freaking Starr.* How was I in the same building with all of these music icons?!? Even the audience was filled with stars: Alice Cooper, Jerry Lee Lewis, Yoko Ono!

Then the moment came. Green Day's video began playing on the big screen with highlights from the band's career. The entire place erupted. The guys played and kicked ass. They screamed through *American Idiot*, *When I Come Around* and *Basket Case*. When Billie Joe, Mike and Tré gave their acceptance speeches, I teared up.

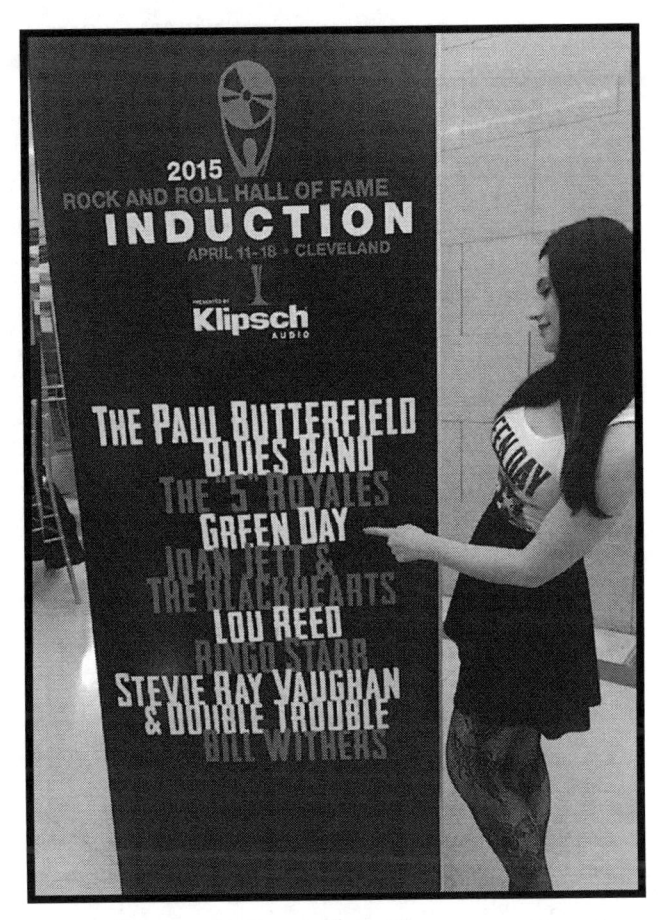

Bethany Moriah, Connecticut.

Then, Sir Paul McCartney took the stage and inducted Ringo Starr. I lost my shit when Ringo invited Green Day back on stage to play the song *Boys*. Fucking Green Day and a Beatle... together?!? Then the stage filled with the rest of the inductees. They played *With a Little Help From My Friends* and *I Wanna be Your Man*. Surreal. The show clocked in at over five hours. I will never forget the night, the show or my friends. We came together to watch history being made.

I love all of you *Idiots!*"

Melissa and
Aaron Cometbus

Melissa Karmel

"When I got to the airport in Cleveland the day after Green Day's induction, a security guard asked if he could help me with anything. I told him to tell me if he saw anyone famous. He laughed. I was looking for Green Day. Then this guy comes in line and shows security his boarding pass. The security guard gasped,

'Oh my God! You're Aaron Cometbus!'

The security guard turned to me and laughed, 'He's famous!'

I said, 'Woooot! OMG.'

I had no idea who he was. I asked him where he was from and he said,

'I don't know how long you have to live in New York to say you're from there, but I live there now. I'm originally from the Bay area.'

I asked, 'Did you go to Green Day's induction?'

He said, 'Yes.'

As he's putting on his punk-ass belt he removed for security, I asked, 'What band are you in?'

He replied, 'I'm not in one. I'm just a...a friend.'

Then he told me that Green Day's roadies were at the airport. So I went looking for them. When I came back, Aaron and I talked. I told him I saw Tim Armstrong and Bill Schneider from Pinhead Gunpowder the night before. He kept smiling and kind of laughing at me. We are about to board, when I saw a picture of him on my news feed. I went to show him and he said,

'That's me. I wonder who was with me? I know who's standing next to me. That's my friend's son.'

That's when I realized he was walking to the Red Carpet. He laughed and then it hit me. I said,

'That's John Kiffmeyer's son. WAIT. WHO ARE YOU?!?' YOU'RE AARON! OMG! YOU WRITE ALL THE SONGS FOR PINHEAD GUNPOWDER, RIGHT?'

He shook his head up and down.

'I LOVE YOU-I HATE-YOU-WHY-DIDN'T-YOU-TELL-ME!'

We had a selfie shoot and he said,

'Let's board and we can talk after the plane lands.'

He signed my notebook and wrote 'To Melissa: Want to hear your songs next time!'

After the flight, he waited for me to come off the plane and gave me some free swag he got at the Rock and Roll Hall of Fame. I told him I was glad he'd waited to tell me who he was so that I could talk to him without *fan-girling*.

He's the coolest motherfucker I've ever met."

From left: Jeff Matika's wife, Janine (Desensitized Brat) and Jeff Matika.

Jeff Matika's wife and Janine's sister.

Mike and Carrie Masterson, New York.

From left: Stacey Vlock, Traci Roll Schaum and Maria Deas.

Billie Joe and Taylor Bellville.

Taylor Bellville

"Dookie was my very first CD. I got it when I was in second grade. The first time I saw Green Day live was during the 2013 *99 Revolutions* tour. I went to Pittsburgh a day early to make sure I'd be first in line. Parking across the street from the venue, I kept watch and finally got in line at 6 a.m. For the next 15 hours, I bonded with my fellow concertgoers.

When the doors opened, I ran to front row center. I'd heard that Billie Joe hadn't been singing *Good Riddance* during the tour. That song means so much to me. I screamed for him to play it and, unbelievably, he heard me. Even as the stage was being broken down, he came over and sang right in front of me.

During the Rock and Roll Hall of Fame weekend, I was able to meet Billie Joe again. He signed my shoulder then stole my Sharpee! I wanted to get his signature permanently tattooed. I slept sitting up, so I didn't smear it. I was so nervous about persevering the signature, that I even had a nightmare that the person I was with washed it off out of jealousy!

The next morning I found a tattoo shop. Now, I have the memory. And, when bad days come along, I don't read the bible, I listen to Green Day."

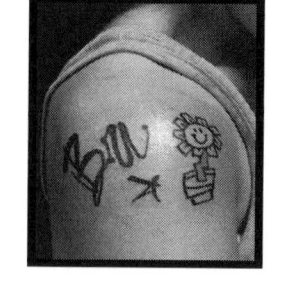

Taylor's tattoo.

Javiera Muñoz, Chile.

Meghan E Tierney and Stephanie Vera-Tudela.

Photo: Taylar Kent

Photo: Sarah Lemke

Photo: Taylar Kent

Special Thanks to Donors Who Made This Edition Possible:

LOVE HAPPENED HERE ON MAY 5,

Sandy Hickman Barber

Ingrid and Kari Bruheim.

Justin Behrle and Marley
by Barbara Bagg.

Nikki DiClementi
(With *Whatsersname* from the touring cast of *American Idiot*, middle, and sister Jena DiClementi, right.)

Desensitized Brat
(Janine!)

Kat Hildebrand
(With Fallyn Ruzzi, left, and Mike Dirnt's wife,
Britnney Cade Dirnt, center.)

Ellie Aronow Hirschfeld

Jayne Hopkins and her daughter, Kerrie Roach.

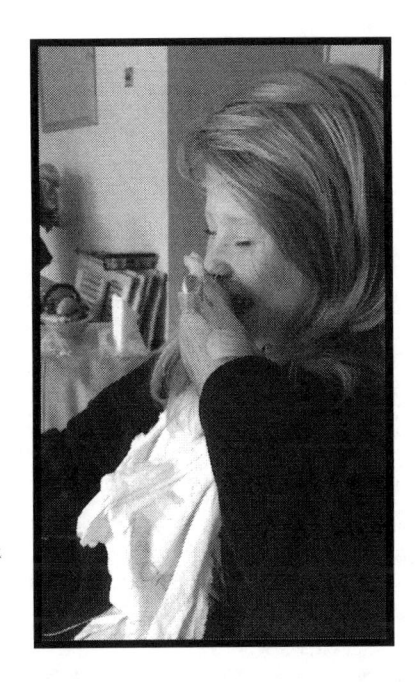

Kerrie's reaction to seeing her photo in the first edition of *Seize the Green Day for the Rock and Roll Hall of Fame.*

Kahla Hutchcroft

Mike Milstine

Eileen Pretzel

Catherine Rock

Traci Schaum. (With Karen Barker.)

Molly and Jim Singerling.

Katie Sullivan

Courtney Trewartha

Vanessa Schuler Verhagen

Deb Wilkinson

Suzanne Wisse with husband Billy.

Hanna Young with Billie Joe Armstrong's nephew Andrew Humann.

Hey-Oh!

♥